Corporate PACs
and
Federal Campaign
Financing Laws

Recent Titles from QUORUM BOOKS

Corporate PACs and Federal Campaign Financing Laws

Use or Abuse of Power?

Ann B. Matasar

QUORUM BOOKS

NEW YORK • WESTPORT, CONNECTICUT • LONDON

Library of Congress Cataloging-in-Publication Data

Matasar, Ann B.
  Corporate PACs and federal campaign financing laws.

  Bibliography: p.
  Includes index.
  1. Campaign funds—United States.   2. Corporations—
United States—Political activity.   3. Political action
committees—United States.   4. Business and politics—
United States.   I. Title.
JK1991.M28   1986   324.7'8'0973   85–12280
ISBN 0–89930–086–3 (lib. bdg. : alk. paper)

Library of Congress Catalog Card Number: 85–12280
ISBN: 0–89930–086–3

First published in 1986 by Quorum Books

Greenwood Press, Inc.
88 Post Road West, Westport, Connecticut 06881

Printed in the United States of America

The paper used in this book complies with the
Permanent Paper Standard issued by the National
Information Standards Organization (Z39.48–1984).

10 9 8 7 6 5 4 3 2 1

CONTENTS

TABLES

FOREWORD

Since the early 1970's, revolutionary changes have occurred in the laws governing contributions to candidates for federal office. These changes accelerated through the late 1970's and are very likely to continue into the 1990's. But while the goal of the 1970's law changes was primarily to limit favoritism and undue influence through requirements for greater public disclosure and limits on both expenditures and contributions, the real outcome of this revolution has been to force candidates to broaden their financial base for sources of additional campaign funds, and to give rise to the growth of corporate political action committees.

In this book, Dr. Ann Matasar examines the formation and activities of corporate political action committees brought on by the revolution in the laws of campaign finance. Because the potential for thousands of additional corporate PACs exists, a decision by these thousands of companies to form new PACs could fundamentally change the nature and outcome of federal elections. Nevertheless, Dr. Matasar's research of the activities of existing business PACs, and her analysis of replies to questionnaires addressed to large business organizations without PACs, has led her to conclude that concerns about the growth of business PACs are unwarranted.

This research also reveals that among other things, corporate PACs are generally risk averse; they avoid the advice of political experts in favor of corporate instincts; they do not concentrate contributions; they overlook uncommitted incumbents and open seat races; and they favor Republicans. Thus by their actions, many corporate PACs miss many opportunities to increase their impact and influence. Dr. Matasar's research sheds new light on the activities and impact of corporate political action committees, while confirming the widely held belief that corporate PACs do abide by the spirit and the letter of the campaign reform laws.

It is appropriate that this study is being published as Congress once again considers legislation to reduce the ceiling on PAC contributions. Dr. Matasar's study of data filed with the Federal Election Commission also provides concrete evidence that the so-called loopholes for bypassing contribution ceilings are not being used, and that contribution ceilings are rarely met by corporate PACs.

This book provides an interesting and fresh look at the changes in Federal campaign laws that gave rise to corporate political action committees, and of the activities of corporate PACs. Her book should be must reading for anyone either associated with a corporate PAC, or contemplating establishing one. The many tables of research data found in the book should also be of interest to Congress, which seems compelled to constrain the activities of PACs without proper consideration of the facts concerning their activities. We are indebted to Dr. Matasar for this important new study.

John D. Tyson,
Vice President of Public Affairs, BATUS Inc.,
and Past-Chairman of the Public Affairs Council

Corporate PACs
and
Federal Campaign
Financing Laws

1

INTRODUCTION

Corporate political action committees (PACs) are a phenomenon of the last fourteen years. They arose from the convergence of two distinct trends in American society during the early 1970s. The first was the desire for campaign finance reform which imbued the decisions and actions of all three branches of the federal government. This resulted in legislation and executive and judicial interpretations which modified, but did not mollify, public suspicion regarding the financial participation of the business community in federal election campaigns, particularly in the post-Watergate era. The second was the corporate responsibility movement which called for greater social and political awareness on the part of management. This resulted in a clearer managerial perception of the integral relationship between business and its external environment and prompted managers to take a more pro-active role in the formation of public policy affecting their firms.

Most managers were reluctant and unskilled political participants. Nonetheless, several factors in the 1970s prodded them into political action in order to protect the interests of their firms and the corporate community in general. The growth in government regulation and its extension into almost every facet of business activity forced managers to become knowledgeable about political and legal affairs in order to remain in compliance with the law. Additionally, new forms of regulations that crossed industrial lines such as health and safety standards were often insensitive to specific requirements of an industry and created complications and resentments within management ranks and a desire to avoid further governmental intervention.

The changing composition of the electorate in conjunction with a rise in general voter apathy also created political conditions of concern to management. Passage in 1971 of the Twenty-sixth Amendment granting suffrage to eighteen-year-olds who maintained the antibusiness bias of the 1960s and the one man, one vote rulings which reduced the legislative representation of conservative rural voters caused the political pendulum to swing against business at all governmental levels. These new conditions proved fertile for the rise of independent and public interest organizations, many of which were antagonistic to business and particularly to large corporations.

In response to these political challenges, many corporations took advantage of legislative reforms regarding the financing of federal election campaigns and established separate segregated funds, commonly called political action committees or PACs, for the collection of voluntary donations from shareholders and selected employees to be used to make contributions to candidates for federal offices. This created a storm of controversy.

Although critics of corporate PACs do not deny their legality, they level criticisms at their legitimacy, methodology, and benefit to the political process. Among the more frequent accusations leveled at these PACs are the following:

1. Corporate PACs foster legalized corruption. This occurs because lawmakers become dependent on them as an easily available source for obtaining substantial sums of money to finance increasingly expensive campaigns and to provide an improved chance of winning.[1]

   Interestingly, some critics reverse this argument and claim that a PAC fosters corruption by making a corporation hostage to unscrupulous politicians who know that the corporation is vulnerable to government pressure "because of the web of federal subsidies, federal taxes, and federal regulations in which they are ensnared and because the federal government is often a primary paying customer for their services and products."[2]

2. Corporate PACs as well as PACs in general have catalyzed and benefited from the decline of political parties and the diluted representation

of constituents by their legislators. Thus PACs have stimulated voter apathy by undermining the party organizations which had traditionally educated voters and brought them to the polls and by making the citizenry cynical regarding the importance of voting for members of Congress.

3. Corporate PACs as well as PACs in general undermine the democratic process and exacerbate the decline in national unity regarding economic and ideological issues by strengthening smaller, specialized interests which work in opposition to the larger public interest and by drowning out the voice of the individual who cannot compete with concentrated wealth.[3]

4. Corporate PAC financial support of candidates buys access and thus influence. Incumbents, in particular, benefit from this system; therefore, they have a self-interest in maintaining the status quo.[4]

5. Corporate PACs provide corporations with an indirect conduit for channeling corporate funds into federal election campaigns, thus bypassing the intent, if not the wording, of the laws prohibiting direct corporate financial involvement.[5]

Herbert Alexander has noted that the attempt to reconcile the inequalities of the distribution of economic resources with the concept of one man, one vote in a democracy is the basic problem of money in politics.[6] Critics of corporate PACs believe the two cannot be reconciled. They remain convinced that money and political power are either synonymous or very closely aligned; therefore, those individuals or groups with money are bound to gain undue representation in the political process and ultimately silence opposition. This position was stated eloquently by Judge J. Skelly Wright of the Eleventh Circuit Court of Appeals:

As individuals are squeezed out, as the behemoths of concentrated wealth dwarf the individual and bid fair to dominate the political field, the very purpose of direct democracy is defeated, and voters are bound to become disillusioned and apathetic. This picture might not trouble a convinced pluralist who sees democratic government as nothing more than the results of the pull and tug of aggregated interests in a field of political vectors and partisan forces of greater or lesser intensity. But I believe in the role of equal individuals in the process of American self-government, and I am convinced that this role cannot be snuffed out without at the same time destroying the integrity of our electoral process and the essence of our political faith.[7]

PACs, including corporate ones, also have their protagonists. Defenders of corporate PACs include those who question the exclusion of corporations from direct involvement in federal election campaign financing as well as those who view PACs as a vehicle for the enhancement of democratic pluralism. Their most frequent claims on behalf of corporate PACs are that:

1. Corporate PACs as well as other forms of PACs represent individuals who share a common set of beliefs and values and can find greater individual expression together through collective action. PACs, therefore, provide legitimate, organized interest representation for individuals.[8]

2. PACs enable candidates without personal wealth or partisan support or both to seek office and have a chance of winning. This enriches political debate and truly opens up the democratic process for more diverse citizen participation.[9]

3. Corporate PACs and the rules that govern them (e.g., disclosure requirements) have brought corporate political involvement into the light for all to see. This adds legitimacy to corporate political activity and increases public faith in our political system.

4. PACs enhance debate and competition of ideas in politics by raising issues (e.g., free enterprise) that are otherwise ignored by political parties.[10]

5. Corporate PACS have helped to balance the overwhelming political power of organized labor.[11]

Both sides of the corporate PAC debate are able to offer examples to support their position. This study, however, asserts that neither side presents an accurate picture of corporate PAC activity. Rather, the reluctance for involvement and lack of political skill which keep most managers out of politics color their managerial activities and make their management of corporate PACs largely ineffective. Thus corporate PACs are not as harmful as critics suggest nor as advantageous as proponents claim.

Four behavioral areas will be analyzed:

1. The manner by which corporate PACs raise funds and the degree to which they seek to maximize the monies available to them for distribution to candidates;

2. The extent to which campaign contribution ceilings are used as well as the importance of contribution patterns in dominating federal officeholders, particularly members of Congress;

3. The degree of coordination among corporate PACs and other business PACs in order to circumvent the contribution limitations and expand their cumulative influence; and

4. The extent to which corporate PACs avoid contribution limitations entirely by using independent expenditures, an unlimited form of freedom of expression.

Additionally, the behavior of corporate PACs will be analyzed from the vantage point of the successful and corporately responsible manager. Thus this work will serve as a guide for corporate PAC policymakers who want their PAC to be politically effective without incurring adverse public reaction.

The data for this study come predominantly from materials and public records published by the Federal Election Commission for the 1978, 1980, and 1982 elections as well as preliminary figures for 1984. For this information I am greatly indebted to Patricia Klein and the staff in the FEC's Records Division. Their friendly and prompt assistance and technical guidance were invaluable.

Special emphasis throughout this work is concentrated on the major corporations in the United States as represented by the listings in *Fortune* magazine. The three *Fortune* lists which served as the basis for the selection of corporations to be studied were the 1983 *Fortune* 500 Largest Industrial Firms (May 2, 1983), the 1982 *Fortune* Second 500 Largest Industrial Firms (June 14, 1982), and the 1983 *Fortune* 500 Largest Nonindustrial or Service Firms (June 13, 1983). Information regarding these firms was obtained from questionnaires sent to them, the FEC, selected interviews, and secondary sources. For the wealth of information derived from this latter group of readings, I am particularly indebted to Carol Barry and other members of the library staff at Elmhurst College where I conducted my research with the assistance of a grant from the Alumni Association. Mrs. Barry's deep interest in my work and her professional commitment and skill brought to my attention and use a vast amount of information.

Others to whom I also owe my thanks are Kay Dabrowski, my administrative assistant at Elmhurst, who coordinated the mailing of the questionnaires and my student assistants, Lynn Coletta and Kim Endres, who aided me with all computer-related analysis. Finally, there is my family—husband, Bob, son, Seth, and daughter, Toby—without whose encouragement, support, love, and understanding none of this would have been possible.

NOTES

1. "Keep Business Cash Out of Politics?" *U.S. News and World Report*, 86, no. 17 (April 30, 1979), p. 53.

2. William T. Mayton, "Politics, Money, Coercion and the Problem with Corporate PACs," *Emory Law Journal*, 29 (Spring 1980), pp. 381–382.

3. For a detailed and impassioned presentation of this view, the reader is directed to Amitai Etzioni, *Capital Corruption* (San Diego: Harcourt Brace Jovanovich, 1984).

4. "Keep business Cash Out of Politics?" p. 54.

5. J. Skelly Wright, "Money and the Pollution of Politics: Is the First Amendment an Obstacle to Political Equality?" *Columbia Law Review*, 82, no. 4 (May 1982), p. 614.

6. Herbert E. Alexander, *Financing Politics: Money, Elections and Political Reform*, 2d ed., Politics and Public Policy Series (Washington, D.C.: Congressional Quarterly Press, 1980), p. 1.

7. Wright, "Money and the Pollution of Politics," p. 625.

8. M. Margaret Conway, "PACs, the New Politics, and Congressional Campaigns," in *Interest Group Politics*, ed. Allan J. Cigler and Burdette A. Loomis (Washington, D.C.: Congressional Quarterly Press, 1983), p. 139.

9. Bernadette A. Budde, "The Practical Role of Corporate PACs in the Political Process," *Arizona Law Review*, 22, no. 2 (1980), p. 557.

10. Stuart Rothenberg, *Campaign Regulation and Public Policy: PACs, Ideology, and the FEC* (Washington, D.C.: The Free Congress Research and Education Foundation, 1981), pp. 44–45.

11. "Keep Business Cash Out of Politics?" p. 53.

2

SETTING THE LEGAL STAGE FOR CORPORATE PACS: A HISTORICAL PERSPECTIVE

U.S. history is replete with examples of corporate involvement in campaign financing and attempts by Congress to prohibit or to control this activity. Since 1907, federal statutes have prohibited direct financial involvement by corporations in the election of federal officials.[1] Major steps toward curbing the influence of aggregate corporate wealth in the political arena were taken in the post–Civil War period because the great concentration of newly acquired industrial capital was being used to corrupt the political process.

When disclosure laws proved unsuccessful in halting this activity, political reformers led by Elihu Root in 1894 and Teddy Roosevelt in 1905 pushed for a total ban on corporate contributions to any political committee or for any political purpose. Their efforts culminated in the Tillman Act of January 26, 1907 (34 Stat. 864 (1907)), which forbade monetary contributions by corporations in federal elections. Within three years Congress passed additional legislation requiring disclosure by committees and organizations seeking to influence federal elections in two or more states to the House of Representatives. This disclosure which included contributions and disbursements as well as the identity of the donors and of the recipients was amended in 1911 to include nominations and elections to the Senate, too.[2]

The Tillman Act was revised, and the legislation of 1910 and 1911 was repealed by the Federal Corrupt Practices Act of 1925

(43 Stat. 1074 (1925)). In *Newberry v. U.S.*, 256 U.S. 232 (1921), the Supreme Court forbade congressional regulation of primaries because they were unknown when the Constitution was adopted. Consequently, the Federal Corrupt Practices Act (FCPA) applied only to federal, general elections.[3] Despite this narrowness of focus, the FCPA extended the monetary contribution prohibitions of the Tillman Act to gifts of valuable property other than money or in-kind services.[4] Additionally, the prohibitions were made applicable to national banks as well as corporations established by national charter. The intent of the Tillman Act and of the FCPA was twofold: to protect the political process from the undue influence of economic interests and thus a loss of its own integrity either perceived or real and to protect corporate minority shareholders against "having monies invested by them in the enterprises used by management to finance political candidates or causes which they opposed."[5] The latter, however, has never been viewed as a compelling governmental interest by itself.[6]

Until 1971 no further major legislation was enacted regarding corporate involvement in the financing of federal election campaigns. In the intervening years, particularly during the 1940s, legislation was passed to include prohibitions on the political activity of labor unions. The War Disputes Act (Smith-Connally Act) of 1943 temporarily extended the prohibitions of the FCPA to unions as well as corporations.[7] This became a permanent feature of the law with the passage of the Labor Management Relations Act (Taft-Hartley Act) of 1947. Prohibitions placed on corporate and union financial involvement in the federal election process also were expanded by the act to cover the nominating process including primaries and conventions. This was made possible by the Supreme Court's decision in *U.S. v. Classic*, 331 U.S. 299 (1941), which negated *Newberry v. U.S.* In 1948 all of the laws governing direct financial participation by labor and corporations in federal election campaigns were codified as Title 18 U.S.C. §610.[8]

Nonetheless, the role of corporations and labor unions as political financiers continued to flourish in an indirect fashion because of the Supreme Court's decision in *U.S. v. C.I.O.*, 335 U.S. 106 (1948), which held that the prohibitions on the use of general or treasury funds did not apply to *segregated* funds which could be used to support political policies and candidates. Additionally, general funds were permitted to be used to express a political viewpoint.[9]

The Federal Election Campaign Act (FECA) of 1971 (P.L. 92–225 (1972)), which became effective on April 7, 1972, amended Title 18 U.S.C. §610, repealed the Federal Corrupt Practices Act of 1925 and Revenue Act of 1971, and codified the "unwritten rules governing political action committees [PACs or] (separate segregated funds) maintained by corporations and labor unions."[10] The original goals of FECA (1971) were to "render the media more accessible and less expensive to candidates for federal office" and to "obtain broad disclosure of federal campaign funds" in an attempt "to discourage the solicitation and acceptance of large sums of money from single contributions."[11]

The goal of reducing expenses was to be attained through a detailed series of limitations placed on candidates' media expenditures at various stages of the election cycle and by placing restrictions on the amount of money that a candidate and members of the immediate family were permitted to contribute to the candidate's own campaign. Disclosure was to be obtained through a series of reports required of candidates and their committees and of committees making political contributions. These complex reports were required to identify those donating $100 or more to a political committee and to be submitted by several specific dates within each year.[12]

To view FECA (1971) in terms of its original intent, however, is too narrow. It also established specific contribution and spending limits for federal candidates and broadened the definition of the term *election* to incorporate general, specific, primary, runoff, nominating convention, and caucus stages of the election process.[13] The terms *contribution* and *expenditure*, however, were redefined to exclude any communications, nonpartisan registration, and get-out-the-vote drives aimed at stockholders and their families, or the establishment, administration, and solicitation of voluntary contributions to a separate segregated fund to be used for political purposes.

These exclusionary provisions were added to FECA (1971) at the urging of organized labor and under the sponsorship of Rep. Orville Hansen of Idaho. Unions were concerned that an adverse decision in the pending case of *Pipefitters Local Union No. 562 v.*

U.S., 407 U.S. 385 (1972), would curtail their practice of mandating contributions from union dues and assessments for separate segrated funds controlled by union officers for political giving. They took a calculated risk that the corporate community, which was given the same privilege, would not be attracted to the use of separate segregated funds.[14] The unions accurately calculated the need for the Hansen amendment in order to win a favorable decision in *Pipefitters*[15] but severely underestimated corporate reaction to PACs.

Although a few corporations had assumed the propriety of using their treasury funds to support a separate segregated fund prior to 1972, passage of FECA (1971) provided the imprimatur of the federal government and the legal clarity which stimulated the formation of a rising number of corporate PACs. The psychological and legal strictures were reduced despite the continued prohibition against corporate direct financial involvement in federal election campaigns.[16]

The explosive growth of corporate PACs, however, is largely a result of the amendments made to FECA in 1974. This legislation (P.L. 93–443 (1975)), which was a reaction to the abuses of Watergate, was considerably more comprehensive than was FECA (1971). Passed on October 15, 1974, and intended to go into effect on January 1, 1975, FECA (1974) did not become operational until April 14, 1975, when the first appointees to the Federal Election Commission (FEC) took office. [17]

FECA (1974) contained many notable provisions which affected all participants in the funding of federal election campaigns. Specifically, it called for (a) the establishment of a six-member, bipartisan FEC to administer the election laws; (b) the amendment of the Internal Revenue Code to create a system of partial or full financing of all stages of the presidential election process; (c) the designation of one central campaign committee by each candidate in order to focus responsibility for compliance and the filing of disclosure reports; (d) the imposition of spending ceilings on campaigns for all federal offices; (e) the prohibition of cash contributions in excess of $100 or foreign contributions of any amount; and (f) the retention of a candidate's self-financing limits and the addition of limits on independent expenditures on behalf of candidates.[18]

Although significant, these features of FECA (1974) had little direct applicability to the growth potential of corporate PACs per se which instead was fostered by two additional features of the law. The first was an amendment to 18 U.S.C. §611 which specifically permitted the establishment of separate segregated funds by government contractors, thus resolving an apparent contradiction with 18 U.S.C. §610 which forbade government contractors' direct or indirect contributions in federal election campaigns. The avoidance of the possible loss of or ineligibility for a contract from the government made many companies less apprehensive about setting up a PAC.

The second feature of FECA (1974) that stimulated the corporate PAC movement was the two-tiered limitation for contributions. Individuals were permitted to contribute no more than $1,000 per candidate per portion of the election cycle and were subject to an aggregate or cumulative ceiling of $25,000. PACs and other political committees by contrast had a $5,000 restriction per candidate per portion of the election cycle and were unlimited in the aggregate. To qualify for these more liberal regulations, a committee had to be classified as achieving multicandidate status which would occur if it was in existence for at least six months, received voluntary contributions from fifty or more persons, and gave contributions to five or more candidates for federal office. While reducing the ability of large personal contributors to dominate the political process, this portion of the law swung the pendulum toward increased influence for organized groups including corporate PACs.

Whatever doubts remained among even the most cautious managers regarding the legality, if not the propriety or wisdom, of corporate PACs were eradicated on November 18, 1975, by the FEC's Advisory Opinion for the Sun Oil Company (AO 1975–23). The company had asked the FEC to clarify if it could use general corporate treasury funds to establish, administer, and solicit money on behalf of a PAC (SUN-PAC) and of a trustee plan (SUN-EPA) into which employees placed funds voluntarily and allowed them to be given by the company as political contributions to candidates chosen by the donor, not the company. Initial reactions of the FEC staff were negative, but they sought confirmation of their position from the Department of Justice.

In a letter dated November 3, 1975, Assistant Attorney General Richard L. Thornburgh told John G. Murphy, general counsel of the FEC, that the Department of Justice took exception to the FEC's position. Regarding SUN-EPA, he said that so long as the company in no way suggests to the contributors to whom they should direct their contributions, pressures them to contribute, or funnels corporate funds indirectly into a campaign, the disbursement of corporate funds to administer the trustee program would be a permissible, nonpartisan activity under 18 U.S.C. §610.

Mr. Thornburgh also defended the company's activities on behalf of SUN-PAC by claiming that the nonpartisan activities added to section 610 by the Hansen amendment were a codification of case law at that point in time and were not intended to exclude other forms of nonpartisan activity. Additionally, he stated that prohibiting a corporation from defraying the political expenses of a PAC would be tantamount to an infringement of the First Amendment rights of employees to associate freely and to express themselves politically. He capped his remarks by saying that his office would not prosecute any company under 18 U.S.C. §610 for activities of the type being conducted by Sun Oil.[19]

In light of the Department of Justice rebuttal, the FEC reconsidered its position and by a 4 to 2 vote confirmed the legality of the activities of Sun Oil. Specifically, the advisory opinion approved Sun Oil's right to:

1. "Expend general treasury funds to defray expenses incurred in establishing, administering and soliciting contributions to SUN-PAC [or SUN-EPA] so long as it is maintained as a separate segregated fund";
2. Solicit "contributions to SUN-PAC from stockholders and employees of the corporation";
3. "Control and direct the disbursement of contributions and expenditures from SUN-PAC"; and
4. Establish multiple PACs, each of which had separate contribution and expenditure limits, so long as their monies were derived solely from voluntary contributions.[20]

The SUN-PAC Advisory Opinion catalyzed the expansion of the corporate PAC movement. Companies no longer needed to be concerned about the legality of underwriting all administrative expenses of a PAC, now had the ability to circumvent contribution ceilings by establishing several PACs to parallel their geographic or divisional structure, and finally had an authorized indirect route for the financing of federal political campaigns via the PAC which could serve as an "alter ego" whose disbursements could be controlled. Effectively, this advisory opinion provided corporate PACs with a wider constituency from which to draw contributions to their coffers and proliferation privileges which potentially allowed for unlimited contributions in federal election campaigns.

Remaining fears of management regarding suits that could be brought against them by disgruntled minority shareholders were alleviated by the Supreme Court's decision in *Cort v. Ash*, 422 U.S. 66 (1975), which "held that no private right of action for damages existed under section 610 for corporate shareholders."[21]

Freedom of corporate PAC activity was expanded further by the Supreme Court in *Buckley v. Valeo*, 424 U.S. 1 (1976), which challenged several portions of FECA (1974) and had broad implications for the federal election process in general. At issue were the constitutionality of contribution and independent expenditure ceilings, disclosure requirements, the method of appointment of the FEC members, federal funding of presidential elections, and the self-financing provisions restricting contributions from a candidate or the candidate's family to his or her own campaign.

In its per curiam opinion, the Court attempted to balance Congress's rights to protect the electoral process from corruption and undue influence as established in *Burroughs and Cannon v. U.S.*, 290 U.S. 534 (1934), [22] and the First Amendment freedoms of expression and association. These issues were resolved in the following manner:

1. All limitations placed upon independent expenditures by individuals and committees in section 608(e) (1) were struck down. These restrictions represented "substantial rather than merely theoretical restraints on the quantity and diversity of political speech." Additionally, inasmuch as they precluded prearrangement and coordination with the candidate or his agent, the corruption danger from *quid pro quo* agreements also was absent.[23] Arguments that unlimited spending would be advantageous to the wealthy over the poor were disregarded because "the concept that government may restrict the speech [i.e., spending]

of some elements of our society in order to enhance the relative voices of others is wholly foreign to the First Amendment."[24]

2. Contribution ceilings for individuals and committees in section 608(b) were upheld. Despite a stated concern that monetary restrictions in a campaign could lower the quality of expression, the depth of exploration, the size of the audience, and the right of citizens to receive information, the Court found contribution limits "only a marginal restriction upon the contributor's ability to engage in free communication." It distinguished between a contribution where the act itself is the indirect, symbolic expression or communication that is unaltered by the amount contributed and an expenditure which is a direct expression and communication and thus is determined by the amount expended. The actual speech associated with a contribution is made by the recipient, not the donor; whereas, with an expenditure, the person or group expending the funds does so to make a definite statement. Finally, it was determined that contribution ceilings had the added benefit of assisting the government in avoiding corruption and the appearance thereof.

3. All self-financing restrictions placed upon candidates and their families under section 608(a) were found to be unconstitutional violations of the First Amendment.

4. Ceilings imposed on expenditures in congressional campaigns in section 608(c) were voided while those placed on presidential campaigns in conjunction with federal funding were supported. This ultimately had the effect of concentrating private funding, including that emanating from corporate PACs, on congressional races.

5. Congressional appointment of four of the six members of the FEC was held to be an unconstitutional violation of the separation of powers.[25]

6. In a footnote the existence of more than one PAC per company was not challenged. The Court let stand the contribution ceilings on a per PAC basis rather than impose a collective constraint for all PACs with a common affiliation.[26]

The Supreme Court in *Buckley* did not address the First Amendment questions underlying the basic prohibition against the direct use of corporate treasury funds in federal election campaigns.[27] Although unresolved at the highest judicial level, this issue had been discussed by a lower court in *U.S. v. U.S. Brewers Association*, 239 Fed. 163 (W.D. Pa. 1916), which found that the Tillman Act's prohibitions against corporate contributions restricted only the spending of money and not freedom of speech because the election process was secured for "natural" rather than "legal" persons who possessed the franchise.[28] It is significant to note, therefore, that although *Buckley* did not deal with this constitutional issue per se, it did alter the relationship of spending and speech and also assumed that the members of the corporate entity—namely, voluntary contributors to its PAC—were appropriate participants in federal election campaigns on a collective as well as individual basis. The most enduring and controversial aspect of *Buckley* may well prove to be its statement that political spending and political speech are inextricably interrelated and that the former cannot be restricted without adversely affecting the latter. Some observers believe that "Rigidly logical extension of the reasoning in *Buckley* and *Bellotti* [to be discussed] would lead to the conclusion that FECA section 441b [which replaced section 610], which presently bans corporate and labor union expenditures in support of a candidate for federal office, is also unconstitutional."[29]

Stung by the SUN-PAC opinion and the *Buckley* decision, Congress quickly reacted by passing amendments to FECA which were signed into law on May 11, 1976. At that time, FECA (1976) (P.L. 94–283 (1976)) was deleted from Title 18 of the U.S. Code and added to Title 2 as sections 431 to 455 (1976). Major features of the new legislation which affected corporations and their PACs included the following.[30]

1. New solicitation rules. Specifically, corporate PACs were restricted in their general solicitation to stockholders, executives and administrative personnel, and the families of these persons. All employees could be solicited for voluntary contributions only through the mail and no more often than twice per year. Methods of solicitation or collection of contributions used by the corporation on behalf of its PAC (e.g., payroll deduction) also had to be made available to the labor unions representing employees in the corporation and had to be noncoercive.

2. Alteration of disclosure requirements. Reports were required from the corporation or its PAC for internal communications costing $2,000 or more and for independent expenditures of $100 or more advocating the election or defeat of a specific candidate. Records had to be maintained of all contributions received by the PAC including the names of donors giving $50 or more. Reports had to be filed with the FEC

providing the names, addresses, and occupations of all contributors of $100 or more to the PAC.

3. Proprietary rights for the corporation in retaining confidentiality of the amount of money it spent in establishing, administering, or soliciting for its PAC. Corporations were permitted to use their PAC as a political alter ego by exercising total control over the PAC's operations without divulging the costs incurred by having the PAC.

4. Disclosure of all contributions to a federal candidate. Honorariums were excluded from the definition of a contribution but were limited to $2,000 plus expenses. Contributions by corporate PACs to national political parties were placed under a $15,000 ceiling.

5. PAC proliferation discouraged. All affiliated committees—those "established, financed, maintained or controlled by the same corporation ... including any parent, subsidiary, branch, division, department, or local unit thereof"[31]—came under one contribution limit as if they were a single PAC of their common "connected organization."[32] The antiproliferation clause (section 441a (a) (5)) established dual standards for determining the existence of a common connected organization for two or more PACs, namely, the Per Se Rule that all PACs created by the same corporation or a part thereof are "per se affiliated" and thus subject to one contribution limit, and the Rule of Reason which goes beyond form to substance and places one contribution limit on PACs which are created, maintained, or controlled by a common entity.[33]

6. Restructured the FEC. All members were to be appointed by the President with the advice and consent of the Senate. Advisory opinions were to be applied to specific issues and not formulated in a general manner.[34]

7. Membership organizations, trade associations, cooperatives, and corporations without stock (e.g., mutual life insurance companies) were authorized to have PACs.[35]

After FECA (1976), the chronology of major events affecting corporate PACs brings us to *First National Bank of Boston v. Bellotti*, 435 U.S. 756 (1978), where the Supreme Court in a 5 to 4 decision held that a corporation could not be restricted in the amount of money it was permitted to spend to influence public sentiment in a referendum. The Court arrived at this conclusion by bringing together three distinct strands of thought regarding the First Amendment. It found that the First Amendment protected the rights of the listener as well as the speaker, that the untrammeled use of the means of communication more than the fostering of equality of access to the means of communication best served the First Amendment, and that commercial speech should be guaranteed First Amendment protection. [36]

Most notable of these findings is the first, in which the justices determined that "the First Amendment goes beyond protection of the press and the self-expression of individuals to prohibit government from limiting the stock of information from which members of the public may draw."[37] The right of the public to be fully informed on an issue meant that all sources of information on the issue, even a corporation, were protected regardless of the possibility as Justice White noted in his dissent that corporate money threatened the "First Amendment as a guarantor of the free marketplace of ideas."[38]

Bellotti (also referred to frequently as *First Boston*) did not extend the direct political use of corporate treasury funds to election campaigns. However, as noted by Justice White, it did "cast considerable doubt upon the constitutionality of legislation passed by some 31 States restricting corporate political activity, as well as upon the Federal Corrupt Practices Act, 2 U.S.C. §441b (1976 ed.)."[39] His argument continued:

If the corporate identity of the speaker makes no difference, . . . the use of corporate funds even for causes irrelevant to the corporation's business, may be no more limited than that of individual funds. Hence, corporate contributions to and expenditures on behalf of political candidates may be no more limited than those of individuals. Individual contributions under federal law are limited but not entirely forbidden.[40]

In a separate dissent, Justice Rehnquist took issue with according a corporation treatment similar to that accorded an individual. He stated that as a creature of the law, a corporation possessed only the privileges conferred by its charter and those incidental to it. Freedom of speech was not a privilege of this type. Additionally, the inability of corporations to speak out freely on any issue would not impair the public's ability to obtain information because individuals within the corporation were free to disseminate their ideas and data.[41]

Many people believe that the *Bellotti* and *Buckley* decisions virtually assure by logical extension that the FCPA ban on the use

of corporate treasury funds as independent expenditures for political purposes will be found to be unconstitutional if and when
it is challenged in court.[42] Whether this same forecast exists for
corporate treasury funds used for direct political contributions is
doubtful. *Bellotti* distinguished between a corporation's right to
speak on issues of general public interest and its participation in
financing political campaigns for election to public office. The
former was defended because it did not carry with it the same
possibilities of corruption through access as did the latter because
the public is less influenced by corporate spending than candidates
might be.[43]

Whereas in *Buckley* the Supreme Court treated contributions
and expenditures differently, in *Bellotti* it gave different treatment
to referenda and candidate elections. After *Bellotti*, therefore, it
appeared that expenditure limits were disallowed in elections and
referenda but that contribution limits were disallowed only in the
latter.[44] Regardless of the final outcome of the debate over the
constitutionality of corporate direct financial involvement in elections, the *Bellotti* decision, by protecting the interests of the public
as hearer rather than the corporation as speaker/spender, makes it
likely that corporate PACs will continue to exist as a legitimate
funnel for corporate political opinion in the federal election
process.[45]

No congressional response resulted from *Bellotti*. In 1979, however, FECA once again was amended. Few of the provisions of
FECA (1979) (P.L. 96–187 (1979)) were of significance to corporate
PACs.[46] Among those with some interest were the reporting
threshold for contributions was raised from $100 to $200 and for
independent expenditures from $100 to $250[47] and the definition
of "standing" which qualified a person or group to seek an advisory
opinion from the FEC was broadened to permit a corporation to
seek information regarding a specific transaction or activity.[48]

The minor revisions in FECA (1979) regarding corporate PACs
reflected an acceptance of them if not a preference. It is not coincidental that the friendlier political environment led to the rapid
expansion of corporate use of this political vehicle.

Since 1971, Congress has sought to reform campaign laws through
a combination of public disclosure, expenditure limits, and contribution restrictions in an attempt to reduce favoritism, corrup-

tion, and the undue influence of certain wealthy persons and organized interests. To a substantial degree these rules have proven most burdensome to small contributors and small campaigns and have enhanced the influence of organized wealth such as that of corporate PACs. Nonetheless, FECA (2.U.S.C. §431 et seq.), the rules and regulations in Title 11 of the Code of Federal Regulations, and the FEC's advisory opinions establish specific parameters for corporate PAC activity, add to the legal burden of companies with PACs, and can complicate the corporation's relations with its many constituencies both within and outside of the firm. To what extent this has curtailed the attractiveness of PACs and their use by the corporate community, particularly its largest members, is the topic of the next chapter.

NOTES

1. T. Richard Mager, "Past and Present Attempts by Congress and the Courts to Regulate Corporate and Union Campaign Contributions and Expenditures in the Election of Federal Officials," *Southern Illinois University Law Journal*, no. 2 (December 1976), p. 339.

2. Margaret T. Murphy McKeown, "A Discussion of Corporate Contributions to Political Campaigns," *Delaware Journal of Corporate Law*, 2, no. 1 (1977), pp. 138–139.

3. *Ibid.*, pp. 139–140.

4. Michael D. Holt, "Corporate Democracy and the Corporate Political Contribution," *Iowa Law Review*, 61 (December 1975), p. 548.

5. Edwin M. Epstein, *Business and Labor in the American Electoral Process: A Policy Analysis of Federal Regulation—The Rise of Political Action Committees*, Institute of Governmental Studies, University of California, Berkeley, August 1978, p. 4.

6. John R. Bolton, "Constitutional Limitations on Restricting Corporate and Political Speech," in *The Corporation in Politics 1981*, Corporate Law and Practice Course Handbook Series, No. 365, ed. Thomas J. Schwarz and Vigo G. Nielsen, Jr. (New York: Practising Law Institute, 1981), p. 470. Some authors believe that the protection of minority stockholders gained importance with the enactment of contribution limitations which precluded undue corporate influence in the political process. Holt, "Corporate Democracy and the Corporate Political Contribution," pp. 556–557. It is noteworthy, however, that in *First National Bank of Boston v. Bellotti*, the Supreme Court specifically rejected minority shareholders' rights as a reason to curb corporate political spending in a ref-

erendum. John G. Murphy, Jr., "The Impact of *First National Bank v. Bellotti*," in *The Corporation in Politics 1979*, Corporate Law and Practice Course Handbook Series, No. 296, ed. Thomas J. Schwarz and Benjamin M. Vandegrift (New York: Practising Law Institute, 1979), p. 50.

7. McKeown, "A Discussion of Corporate Contributions to Political Campaigns," p. 140.

8. Joseph E. Cantor, *Political Action Committees: Their Evolution and Growth and Their Implications for the Political System* (Washington, D.C.: Congressional Research Service, 1981), pp. 21–22.

9. Holt, "Corporate Democracy and the Corporate Political Contribution," pp. 549–550.

10. Benjamin M. Vandegrift and Daniel J. Swillinger, "Contributions and Expenditures," in *The Corporation in Politics 1979*, ed. Schwarz and Vandegrift, p. 59.

11. John Egan, "Affiliation of Political Action Committees under the Antiproliferation Amendments to the Federal Election Campaign Act of 1971," *The Corporation in Politics 1981*, ed. Schwarz and Nielsen, pp. 421–422.

12. Alexander, *Financing Politics: Money, Elections and Political Reform*, pp. 29–30.

13. Stephen H. Fletcher, "Corporate Political Contributions," *The Business Lawyer*, 29, no. 4 (July 1974), p. 1074.

14. Epstein, *Business and Labor in the American Electoral Process*, pp. 11–13.

15. The decision in *Pipefitters* gave unions and corporations the right to make unlimited contributions or expenditures of PAC money as long as that money was derived voluntarily from specific persons aware that it would be used politically. Mager, "Past and Present Attempts by Congress and the Courts," p. 360.

16. There are two other exemptions to this rule. Corporate treasury money may be spent for communications, even of a partisan nature, to shareholders, executives, administrative personnel, and the families of these groups and for nonpartisan registration and get-out-the-vote drives to all personnel. If the latter activities are partisan, they can be directed only to the above-specified groups. Benjamin M. Vandegrift, "The Corporate Political Action Committee," *New York University Law Review*, 55 (June 1980), pp. 425–427.

17. Herbert E. Alexander, *Financing the 1976 Election* (Washington, D.C.: Congressional Quarterly Press, 1979), p. 11.

18. Alexander, *Financing Politics: Money, Elections and Political Reform*, pp. 168–170 for a fuller summary of these provisions.

19. Letter from Assistant Attorney General Richard L. Thornburgh to John G. Murphy, general counsel of the FEC, November 3, 1975.

20. Federal Election Commission, "Advisory Opinion 1975–23," *Federal Register*, 40, no. 233 (December 3, 1975), pp. 56584–56585.

21. Bolton, "Constitutional Limitations on Restricting Corporate and Political Speech," p. 474.

22. Richard Claude and Judith Kirchhoff, "The 'Free Market' of Ideas, Independent Expenditures, and Influence," *North Dakota Law Review*, 57, no. 3 (1981), pp. 338–339.

23. *Buckley v. Valeo*, 424 U.S. 19 and 47 (1976).

24. Wright, "Money and the Pollution of Politics," p. 612.

25. *Buckley v. Valeo*, 424 U.S. 19–21, 26, 27 and 58 (1976).

26. "A business conduit for campaign cash," *Business Week*, no. 2419 (February 16, 1976), p. 25.

27. In *FEC v. Lance* (5th Cir. 1981), a federal appellate court upheld the constitutionality of this prohibition as it applies to national banks and thus by extension to federally chartered corporations. Benjamin J. Vandegrift, "Restrictions on Political Contributions and Expenditures by Business Corporations," in *The Corporation in Politics: PACs, Lobbying Laws, and Public Officials 1983*, ed. Thomas J. Schwarz and Vigo G. Nielsen, Jr. (New York: Practising Law Institute, 1983), pp. 45–46. It should also be noted, however, that corporations and not-for-profit organizations set up with state charters may contribute to federal election campaigns. In twenty-four states it also is legal for corporations to use treasury funds for support of candidates for states offices. John C. Perham, "The New Zest of the Corporate PACs," *Dun's Review*, 115, no. 2 (February 1980), p. 51.

28. Mager, "Past and Present Attempts by Congress and the Courts," pp. 340–342.

29. Archibald Cox. "Constitutional Issues in the Regulation of the Financing of Election Campaigns," *Cleveland State Law Review*, 31 (Summer 1982), p. 406.

30. A more detailed summary of FECA (1976) is found in Alexander, *Financing Politics: Money, Elections and Political Reform*, pp. 171–173.

31. Federal Election Commission, *Corporate-Related Political Committees Receipts and Expenditures*, FEC Disclosure Series No. 8, 1976 Campaign, September 1977, pp. 4–5.

32. Mark Elliott Mazo, "Impact on Corporations of the 1976 Amendments to the Federal Election Campaign Act," *The Business Lawyer*, 32, no. 2 (January 1977), pp. 429–436.

33. Egan, "Affiliation of Political Action Committees," pp. 423–424.

34. Rothenberg, *Campaign Regulation and Public Policy*, p. 5.

35. Edwin M. Epstein, "The Business PAC Phenomenon: An Irony of Electoral Reform," *Regulation*, 3, no. 3 (May/June 1979), p. 37.

36. Francis H. Fox, "Corporate Political Speech: The Effect of First

National Bank of Boston v. Bellotti upon Statutory Limitations on Corporate Referendum Spending," *Kentucky Law Review*, 67, no. 1 (1978–1979), pp. 75–76.

37. *First National Bank of Boston v. Bellotti*, 435 U.S. 783 (1978).

38. *Ibid.*, pp. 776, 777, and 810.

39. *Ibid.*, p. 803.

40. *Ibid.*, p. 821.

41. *Ibid.*, pp. 825–828.

42. Alexander, *Financing the 1976 Election*, pp. 618–619; and Thomas B. Green, "Prohibition of Corporate Political Expenditures: The Effects of *First National Bank v. Bellotti*," in *The Corporation in Politics 1980*, ed. Thomas J. Schwarz and Vigo G. Nielsen, Jr., Corporate Law and Practice Course Handbook Series, No. 329 (New York: Practising Law Institute, 1980), pp. 369–370.

43. Cox, "Constitutional Issues," p. 407; and Albert S. Lagano, "Elections: Corporate Free Speech—The Right to Spend and Contribute, The Right to Influence and Dominate," *Stetson Law Review*, 12 (Fall 1982), p. 241.

44. Eric L. Richards, "The Rise and Fall of the Contribution/Expenditure Distinction: Redefining the Acceptable Range of Campaign Finance Reforms," *New England Law Review*, 18, no. 2 (Spring 1983), p. 381.

45. Marlene Arnold Nicholson, "The Constitutionality of the Federal Restrictions on Corporate and Union Campaign Contributions and Expenditures," *Cornell Law Review*, 65, no. 6 (August 1980), p. 954.

46. For a more detailed synopsis of this law, see Alexander, *Financing Politics: Money, Elections and Political Reform*, pp. 174–176.

47. Herbert E. Alexander, *Financing the 1980 Election* (Lexington, Mass.: Lexington Books, 1983), p. 13.

48. Charles N. Steele, "Enforcement under the 1979 FECA Amendments," in *The Corporation in Politics 1980*, ed. Schwarz and Nielsen, p. 42.

3

DIMENSIONS OF THE CORPORATE PAC PHENOMENON: THE NUMERICAL AND FINANCIAL STRENGTH OF CORPORATE PACS

Those who look with suspicion or apprehension upon the role played by money in the political process have been alarmed by the numerical and financial growth of corporate PACs. Critics assume that the increased participation of these PACs in the election process will serve as a means for the financial strength of the corporate community to be funneled into endless sums of money for candidates for federal office. The corporate community then would come to dominate federal elections and make a mockery of democracy and representative government as we know it. This chapter reviews the historical growth of corporate PACs as well as their future prospects and attempts to determine if the fears of their critics are justified.

The involvement of the corporate community in politics, including campaign financing, is as old as the nation itself. As noted by Edwin Epstein:

Political involvement by economic interests, including business organizations, has been an enduring and inevitable concommittant [sic] both of America's democratic tradition of dispersed societal power, and of the vital importance of governmental policies and decisions to the survival and well-being of virtually every business firm in an interdependent political economy.[1]

This historical reality has not been favored by many Americans. The public's distrust of corporations and displeasure with their direct financial involvement in election campaigns gained a firm legislative foothold in the Tillman Act of 1907 and, subsequently, the Federal Corrupt Practices Act of 1925 as noted in chapter 2. During most of the twentieth century, therefore, corporate financial involvement in federal election campaigns has been undertaken indirectly in the form of corporate communications on issues or candidates or through individual contributions from executives or other persons associated with the corporation.[2] Additionally,

Such election-related activities as voter registration and get-out-the vote drives among employees, provision of employee and stockholder lists to political parties, payroll deduction systems for political contributions, and campaign fund-raising drives among employees were conducted by various corporations, apparently not in violation of 18 U.S.C. 610.[3]

Particularly popular among corporations were trustee accounts—PAC-like organizations through which voluntary contributions were collected from employees regularly, often through payroll deduction, kept in individual bank accounts, and disbursed to candidates in accordance with the specific wishes of the donor. Between 1958 and 1964, fifty firms had bipartisan political fund-raising activities to encourage employee contributions to political parties and candidates.[4] In California, some corporations had PACs in place in order to be politically active at the state rather than federal level.[5] The pre-1971 establishment of corporate PACs was legal at the federal and state levels if no corporate treasury money was used to underwrite or to support the PAC. Table 1 reflects the growth of business-related PACs during the 1960s. These corporate committees grew financially from $16,500 in 1960 to approximately $1.4 million by 1968.[6] Trade associations and business-related interest organizations such as the Business-Industry PAC (BIPAC), however, were more likely to have PACs than were corporations in order to respond to the increased political clout of organized labor after the merger of the AFL-CIO in 1955.[7]

The personal contributions from corporate executives who were surrogates for their companies were of greater importance to the indirect role of corporations in the funding of federal election campaigns. As early as 1956, 199 officials of 225 of the largest

Table 1
Business PAC Growth Prior to 1970

Year	Type of Business PAC			
	Corporate	*Industry*	*General*	*Total*
1960	0	1	0	1
1964	0	6	1	7
1968	5	28	1	34
1970	13	40	2	55

Source: Edwin M. Epstein, *Business and Labor in the American Electoral Process: A Policy Analysis of Federal Regulation—The Rise of Political Action Committees.* Institute of Governmental Studies, University of California, Berkeley, August 1978, p. 9.

corporations gave $1.9 million in amounts of $500 or more to interstate committees. They were able to bypass federal contribution limits by giving cash, contributing only to intrastate committees from which the money could be transferred into interstate campaigns, or using members of their families as conduits.[8] The dimension of this political funding is not known exactly because of the lax enforcement of disclosure laws and the ability of individuals to avoid them and other campaign finance restrictions.

The election of 1972, the first to occur after passage of FECA (1971), marks the point from which the growth of PACs ordinarily is studied. Eighty-seven corporate PACs, approximately eighty of which were established after FECA went into effect in April 1972, were involved in that election.[9] Table 2 shows that the number of corporate PACs rose by only two, from 87 in 1972 to 89 in 1974 when this data commences. From 1974 to 1976, there was modest growth among corporate PACs which could be attributed to the FECA (1974) amendments which repealed the prohibitions against campaign activity by government contractors. Rather than bringing new companies into the political arena, however, the pre-1976 PAC growth among corporations was confined largely to the registration of previously unregistered employee political organizations such as trustee accounts. Corporations without prior plans for employees' campaign donations remained uninvolved in politics for the initial years of FECA's existence. Corporate PACs created prior

Table 2
PAC Growth—From 1974

"PAC" GROWTH—FROM 1974

COMMITTEE TYPE	12/31/74	11/24/76[1]	6/10/76[2]	12/31/76	12/31/77	12/31/78	8/79	12/31/79	7/1/80	12/31/80	7/1/81	12/31/81	7/1/82	12/31/82	7/1/83	12/31/83	7/1/84
CORPORATE	89	139	294	433	550	784	884	949	1,106	1,204	1,251	1,327	1,415	1,467	1,512	1,536	1,639
LABOR	201	226	246	224	234	217	226	240	255	297	303	318	350	380	379	378	381
TRADE/MEMBERSHIP HEALTH	318*	357*	452*	489*	438	451	481	512	542	574	577	608	613	628	641	617	628
NON-CONNECTED					110	165	209	250	312	378	445	539	644	746	765	821	977
COOPERATIVE					8	12	13	17	23	42	38	41	45	47	50	51	53
CORPORATION W/O STOCK					20	24	27	32	41	56	64	68	82	103	114	122	125
TOTAL	608	722	992	1,146	1,360	1,653	1,840	2,000	2,279	2,551	2,678	2,901	3,149	3,371	3,461	3,525	3,803

[1] On November 24, 1975, the Commission issued Advisory Opinion 1975-23 "SUNPAC."

[2] On May 11, 1976, the President signed the Federal Election Campaign Act Amendments of 1976, P.L. 94-283.

*For the years 1974—1976, these numbers represent all other political committees . . . no further categorization is available.

Source: FEC Press Release, August 24, 1984.

to 1975, therefore, had an early start that has aided them in gaining financial strength over the years.[10]

The extraordinary increase in the number of corporations establishing PACs occurred after 1976 as an outgrowth of the SUN-PAC Advisory Opinion and the 1976 amendments to FECA. The changes brought by these two events reduced uncertainty regarding the formation, structure, and administration of a PAC and made it possible for many corporate officials to view PACs in a more positive light and as less risky for their companies.

In the more than nine years from the end of 1974 to mid-1984, the number of corporate PACs rose by 1,550, an 18.5–fold increase. While significant unto itself, this appears particularly startling if compared with the 180 PACs or 1.9–fold increase experienced by labor PACs in the same period or the 867 PACs or 8.9–fold increase of the nonconnected or unaffiliated PACs from 1977, when they were first recorded separately, until mid-1984.

It is also important to note, however, that the growth rate of corporate PACs has peaked. On a relative basis this occurred in 1976 when corporate PACs grew by 487 percent from the prior election. Absolutely the greatest growth among corporate PACs occurred between the 1978 and 1980 elections when 322 new corporate PACs were established. Since 1977, corporate PACs have composed the largest category among all PACs registered with the FEC on an absolute basis. Relatively, however, the corporate PAC category has declined steadily since July 1980 when it represented approximately 49 percent of all PACs.

The rate of PAC formation by *Fortune* companies also has peaked. Among the 500 largest industrial corporations, 202 of them had PACs in place for the 1978 election, and by the 1980 election, there were 286.[11] As of mid-1983 when this study was undertaken, only 12 additional PACs had been established among these *Fortune* companies, bringing the total to 298.[12]

PACs have never been as popular among the second 500 largest industrial firms as among the 500 largest ones. In 1978, only 42 of these firms had established PACs, and by 1980, this number had risen to 68.[13] As of mid-1983, only 81 of these firms had PACs,[14] while 419 of them did not have PACs.

No comparison of a similar nature is possible for the *Fortune* 500 largest nonindustrial or service corporations. Prior to 1983,

Fortune listed only 300 of these companies and categorized them differently. In 1983 *Fortune* divided the nonindustrial list into 100 bank holding companies (BHC); 100 diversified financial services; 100 diversified services; and 50 each of life insurance, retail, transportation, and utility companies. Among these firms 74 BHCs,[15] 42 diversified financial services, 43 diversified services, 23 life insurance companies, 21 retail companies, 30 transportation companies, and 46 utilities had PACs in mid-1983. On a percentage basis, utilities were most likely to have a PAC, followed by BHC, diversified financial services or diversified service companies, transportation companies, life insurance companies, and retail companies. More revealing, however, is the fact that among the utilities, 36 of their firms had PACs dating back as far as 1978 and another 8 dating back to 1980. Only 8 utility companies formed new PACs for the 1982 election. Life insurance firms, by contrast, had only 5 companies with PACs dating back to 1978, 11 dating back to 1980, and 7 which were established for the 1982 election. With the exception of life insurance companies, which have only recently begun to be affected by a changing federal regulatory climate, all categories on this *Fortune* list revealed a declining interest in establishing new PACs after 1978.

Substantial growth potential existed for PAC formation among the *Fortune* corporations that had not established PACs by mid-1983. In order to forecast the extent to which this potential would be achieved, a questionnaire was sent to 760 of these *Fortune* companies. Replies were received from 169 or 22 percent of them. Among the respondents, only 3 intended to establish a PAC; 26 were uncertain; and 140 specifically denied having any plans for establishing a federal PAC. These findings reveal that the great growth era for the formation of corporate PACs is definitely over. If the largest corporations do not develop PACs, it is unlikely that smaller corporations will do so in light of the positive correlation between size and market share and the likelihood that a company will establish a PAC.[16] The continuous and overwhelmingly negative reaction to PAC formation among *Fortune* companies without PACs bodes poorly for the continued growth of the corporate PACs.

Size alone, however, may not fully explain the potential for future PAC growth. Edwin Epstein claimed that two other factors affected the scope and magnitude of corporate political involvement—namely, the degree of government regulation and the "extent to which company business and well-being depend upon governmental decisions."[17] Nonetheless, he noted that the size of the company remained the most important variable affecting corporate political involvement at the national level.

Continued formation of corporate PACs, however, cannot be discounted simply because they are unattractive to many large corporations in which motives for establishing a corporate PAC abound. Corporate managers may succumb to peer pressure either on a regional or industry-wide basis.[18] In small or medium-sized firms, in particular, corporate leaders with deep political commitments may wish to use a PAC to promote a philosophical position. Some companies may want to counterbalance the influence of labor's perceived political strength.[19] Others may wish to extend the arm of their lobby, reduce political solicitation pressures exerted by candidates directly on their top executives, appear to be socially involved and progressive corporate citizens, hope to alter the philosophy of Congress, provide support for specific legislation, or stimulate wider political participation among employees.[20] Finally, a PAC may be viewed as a vehicle for overcoming the lower contribution ceilings placed on wealthy individuals such as some corporate executives.[21]

Despite these arguments, however, the fact remains that most of the nation's largest publicly owned corporations do not have a PAC and appear unlikely to have one in the future for a variety of reasons. Eighty-seven respondents to the questionnaire perceived no need for a PAC because many individuals in their corporation already were financially involved in electoral campaigns or because the political needs of their company were adequately cared for by a trade association PAC. Fifty-seven firms responded that they considered having a PAC to be an inappropriate corporate activity because of the nature of their business which required them to retain an impartial political posture or because of their foreign parentage which compelled them to avoid any implications of improper or illegal activity.[22]

Thirty-six companies refused to have a PAC for fear of alienating employees or shareholders. In particular, managers were concerned that employees would view the PAC as a "shakedown." A desire to avoid developing artificial castes and confusing job definitions through the establishment of the solicitation categories also has been linked to the issue of employee alienation.[23] Ironically, these arguments stand in sharp contrast to the claims that corporate PACs raise the consciousness of employees, foster employee political involvement and citizenship, and help shareholders create a more favorable governmental environment for the corporation.[24]

Thirty-two respondents refused to establish PACs because they were disenchanted with them or believed that they had a negative public image that could tarnish their company's reputation by being affiliated with one. In particular, the "activities of independent PACs of the more right wing conservative groups have scared off many moderate business organizations."[25] As long as the public lumps all PACs together, regardless of category, this problem is likely to discourage many corporations from establishing a PAC.

Thirty-eight companies specifically mentioned the cost of establishing and administering the PAC as a deterrent. Several of them said that the weakened financial condition of their corporation made it inappropriate to divert energy, talent, and money to a PAC. As the rules, regulations, tax questions, and other legal matters related to PACs continue to multiply and become more complex, these costs are likely to increase and to prevent other corporations from establishing a PAC.

The Internal Revenue Service also has increased the administrative costs associated with a corporate PAC. In Technical Advice Memorandum 8202019 issued on September 30, 1981, the IRS stated that administrative expenses incurred by a corporation on behalf of its affiliated PAC are not deductible because they are classified under section 162(e) of the Internal Revenue Code as expenditures incurred in connection with a political campaign.[26] Additionally, "section 162(e) (2) (A) disallows a deduction 'for any amount paid or incurred (whether by way of contribution, gift or otherwise)' for participation in a political campaign"[27] and "section 162(e) (2) (B) together with Regs. §1. 162–20(c) (4) disallows a deduction for expenditures connected with any attempt to influence the general public, or segments thereof, with respect to legislative matters, elections, or referendums."[28]

By eliminating the deductibility of administrative expenses incurred on behalf of a PAC, these memoranda increased the effective

Table 3
Administrative Costs Incurred by *Fortune* Corporations on Behalf of Their
Affiliated PACs

Administrative Costs Incurred	Number of Corporations
$0–$999	25
$1,000–$2,499	8
$2,500–$4,999	7
$5,000–$9,999	13
$10,000–24,999	13
$25,000–$49,999	6
$50,000–$74,999	2
$75,000–99,999	0
$100,000 or more	1

Source: Responses from questionnaires.

or true dollar cost of an affiliated PAC to its connected corporation. In light of these rulings and the substantially fixed nature of the costs associated with a PAC, the expenses of underwriting a PAC may bear more heavily upon companies, especially smaller ones.[29] As fewer large corporations find PACs attractive, these rulings make it likely that smaller companies will be even less inclined to underwrite the costs of a PAC even though their managers consider more forms of political action proper.[30]

The exact cost to a corporation of establishing, administering, and soliciting for its affiliated PAC is proprietary information which does not have to be disclosed. Table 3 reflects responses from seventy-five *Fortune* companies regarding these costs. Thirty-two additional corporations answered that the amounts expended by them on their PACs were nominal, covering items such as postage and printing; but two respondents stated that the amount spent on their company's PAC amounted to approximately fifty cents for every dollar collected on behalf of the PAC. These companies confessed, however, that the amount being spent would be substantially larger if executive or professional time commitments were included. Forty-two companies responding to the questionnaire refused to divulge information regarding administrative costs associated with their PAC because it was undetermined or was to remain confidential.

Many managers are disinclined toward PACs because of their general reluctance to become engaged in political activity of any kind. They continue to believe that "the business of business is business"[31] or that increased corporate political activity will spur unions to greater political activity, polarize the political parties, and blur the distinctions between the public and private realms, thus adversely affecting corporate autonomy.[32]

Because it is still possible for a corporation to have more than one PAC affiliated with it, it is necessary to distinguish between the number of corporate PACs and the number of companies having affiliated PACs. Nonproliferation provisions in FECA (1976) discouraged multiple PACs by putting all PACs with a common affiliation under one contribution ceiling, but they did not prohibit this practice. For those corporations that wish to maximize their influence, multiple PACs can parallel distinct geographic, product, or subsidiary diversity and permit more effective fund-raising activities among targeted groups. Multiple PACs also aid the company in obscuring its accumulated political power because financial disclosure records are listed by the individual PAC rather than the parent corporation.[33]

Despite the advantages for a company which has more than one PAC, only sixty-nine corporations on the *Fortune* lists as shown in the appendixes had established multiple PACs. In many instances they were the by-products of mergers and acquisitions among companies that had established PACs independently. The dearth of multiple PACs among the largest corporations is attributable to several factors including the additional costs associated with having multiple PACs and a managerial preference for an appearance of consolidation and unity in political as well as financial statements emanating from the company.

To what extent the increase in the number of corporate PACs or the number of corporations having PACs is significant in itself is a matter of dispute. Some observers consider the numerical growth of corporate PACs to guarantee positive results for the business community in the political arena.[34] Others see this growth as diffusing the power of corporations and thus defending the political system against the undue influence of the business community.[35]

Regardless of the position to which one subscribes, the fact remains that the explosive growth of corporate PACs on the American political scene is a historical phenomenon which cannot be overlooked.

As noted earlier, however, it is unlikely that the future expansion of the corporate PAC movement will continue at the same rapid pace as it has in the past. A substantial number of the nation's largest companies still refuse to establish PACs, and smaller companies are unlikely to accept the expense or see the need for one. Edwin Epstein's observation—"Impressive as the growth in corporate PACs has been, what is astonishing is how few corporate PACs there are, given how many there might be"—remains true.[36] The potential for greater influence of corporate PACs, however, remains substantial even if their number does not increase because of the internal financial growth potential of each of the existing corporate PACs.

To a considerable degree, the financial growth of existing corporate PACs as well as that of unaffiliated or ideological ones has been more dramatic than the proliferation of PACs. Table 4 reflects the financial growth of all PACs in federal elections from 1972 to 1982 on the basis of dollar contributions to candidates. Because corporate PACs rarely make independent expenditures and can rely upon corporate treasury monies for their expenses and non-partisan, political education activities, contribution figures provide a relatively accurate account of their financial involvement in the political process. The data reveal that corporate PACs have contributed an ever-increasing absolute amount in each subsequent federal election cycle. Nonetheless, the percentage of PAC contributions made by corporate PACs appears to have leveled off since 1980.

Further doubt as to the dominance of corporate PAC contributions in federal election campaigns is created when all sources of campaign funding for congressional candidates is considered as it is in table 5. It is apparent that PACs have remained less important as financial angels than have individual contributors for all federal election campaign cycles. In summary, one can say that "PACs are by no means the dominant element in congressional campaign finance, but their relative importance has clearly grown."[37] Interestingly, this has occurred even though many PACs affiliated

Table 4
Contributions to Congressional Candidates by Political Action Committees, by Category, 1972–82 (in millions)

Type of PAC	1972	1974	1976	1978[a]	1980[a]	1982[a]
Labor	$3.6	$6.3	$8.2	$9.9	$13.2	$20.3
Business-related[b]	2.7	4.4	10.0	–	–	–
Corporate	–	–	–	9.5	19.2	27.5
Trade/member-ship/health	–	–	–	11.2	15.9	21.9
Nonconnected[c]	–	0.7	1.5	2.5	4.9	10.7
Other[d]	2.2	1.0	2.8	1.0	2.0	3.2
TOTAL[e]	$8.5	$12.5	$22.6	$34.1	$55.2	$83.6

NOTE: Data are for all congressional candidates, except for 1972, where primary losers are exclud

SOURCES: For 1972-76, and for footnotes, Cantor, *Political Action Committees,* 87-88. For 19 Federal Election Commission, *Reports on Financial Activity, 1977-78, Interim Rep. No. 5* (U.S. Senate and House Campaigns), June 1979, 94. For 1980, Federal Elect. Commission, *Reports on Financial Activity, 1979-80, Final Report* (U.S. Senate . House Campaigns), January 1982, 127. For 1982, Federal Election Commission, *Rep on Financial Activity, 1981-82, Final Report* (U.S. Senate and House Campaigns), O ber 1983, 92.

a. Contributions to candidates for election in the year indicated, made during the two-y election cycle.

b. This encompasses the Common Cause categories for business, health, and, in 1976, la yers. This category is included here for the purpose of listing the data for 1972-76, bef the specific breakdowns were devised by the FEC for the corporate and other categori and it is based on the assumption that the majority of PACs it includes have a basic probusiness orientation. It is only roughly comparable to the combined corporate a trade/membership/health groups in 1978-82, but most of the business-related PACs wo fall into those two FEC categories (some would be scattered in the nonconnected, operative, and corporation without stock groups).

c. For 1974 and 1976 the nonconnected category, as defined by the FEC, correlates w the ideological group used by Common Cause for those two years. Most of the ideol ical PACs are today listed in the nonconnected group, but the latter also includes PA that are not ideological. Thus the data for 1974 and 1976 are not exactly compara to those for 1978-82, in view of the different standards applied to the nonconnec and the ideological groups. (Ideological PACs in 1972 were lumped into Common Caus "miscellaneous" group.)

d. This is a catchall category, in which the earlier figures are only roughly comparable the later ones. For 1972-76 the data represent Common Cause's "miscellaneous" catego which included such groups as the NEA (and affiliates), environmentalists, and so cooperatives, and its agriculture/dairy category. In 1972 Common Cause included ideological PACs under "miscellaneous," before their separate listing in 1974; thus 19 includes more types of PACs than the 1974 and 1976 data do. For 1978-82 the "oth data equate directly with the FEC's cooperatives and corporations without stock grou Thus the data for 1972 are not exactly comparable with those for 1978-82. The co mon thread is the inclusion of the major dairy PACs—ADEPT, C-TAPE, and SPACE in "other" in all six election years.

e. Figures in columns may not add to totals because of rounding.

Source: Michael J. Malbin and Thomas W. Skladony, "Appendix: Selected Campaign Finance Data," in *Money and Politics in the United States*, ed. Michael J. Malbin (Chatham, N.J.: Chatham House Publishers, Inc., 1984), p. 298.

Table 5
Sources of Campaign Contributions to Major-Party House and Senate General Election Candidates, 1974–82

	1974	1976	1978	1980	1982
House Elections					
Average					
Contribution	$61,084	$79,421	$111,232	$148,268	$222,620
Percentage from:					
Individuals	73	59	61	67[a]	63[a]
Parties[b]	4	8	5	4	6
PACs	17	23	25	29	31
Candidates[c]	6	9	9	–	–
Senate Elections					
Average					
Contribution	$455,515	$624,094	$951,390	$1,079,346	$1,771,167
Percentage from:					
Individuals	76	69	76	78[a]	81[a]
Parties[b]	6	4	2	2	1
PACs	11	15	14	21	18
Candidates[c]	1	12	8	–	–
Source not known	6	–	–	–	–

SOURCES: Compiled from the following sources. For 1974, Common Cause, *1974 Congressional Campaign Finances,* vol. 1 (Washington, D.C., 1976). For 1976, Federal Election Commission, *Disclosure Series No. 9* (House of Representatives Campaigns), September 1977; and *Disclosure Series No. 6* (Senatorial Campaigns), April 1977. For 1978, Federal Election Commission, *Reports on Financial Activity, 1977-78, Interim Report No. 5* (U.S. Senate and House Campaigns). For 1980, Federal Election Commission, *Reports on Financial Activity, 1979-80, Final Report* (U.S. House and Senate Campaigns). For 1982, Federal Election Commission, *Reports on Financial Activity, 1981-82, Interim Report No. 3* (U.S. House and Senate Campaigns).

a. Includes candidates' contributions to their own campaigns, loans, transfers, and other items.

b. Does not include party expenditures in behalf of candidates.

c. Includes candidates' loans unrepaid at time of filing.

Source: Gary C. Jacobson, "Money in the 1980 and 1982 Congressional Elections," in *Money and Politics in the United States,* ed. Michael J. Malbin (Chatham, N.J.: Chatham House Publishers, Inc., 1984), p. 39.

with corporations have chosen not to contribute to any candidates. In the 1982 election cycle, only 1,317 of the 1,557 corporate PACs in existence made any contributions in federal campaigns.[38] Despite their relative position among campaign finance sources, PACs, including those affiliated with corporations, remain a target for critics concerned with the overall cost of election campaigns. PACs collectively are viewed as a stimulus for increased expenditures by candidates who do not have to economize because they can turn to these organizations for larger sources of funds. In fact PACs may have underwritten this financial explosion, but they did not create it. The costs associated with campaigns for federal office, like those for many other factors in our economy, have risen because of inflation. Additionally, campaign costs have been affected by a greater reliance on TV, mass mailings and other costly fund-raising efforts, increased use of computers for campaign analysis and operations, the employment of public opinion pollsters and political consultants, and the need to hire professional staff to comply with a larger number of complex governmental reporting requirements.[39]

In the future, candidates may need to run more efficient campaigns and curb their expenditures because they may not be able to rely on PACs or on individuals to absorb the additional expenses of underwriting their campaigns. As the growth rate in PAC formation diminishes, the ability and willingness of existing PACs to contribute amounts sufficient to meet the greater costs of campaigns is questionable. As shown in chapter 4, corporate PACs are not likely to give individual candidates large sums of money nor to approach the contribution ceilings available to them. If history serves as a guide to the future, corporate PACs will not assist in the unlimited growth of campaign spending.

Ultimately, the future financial growth of corporate PACs will depend on the willingness and ability of existing PACs to solicit larger sums of money than they have in the past without violating the legal strictures governing solicitation. FECA states that "it shall be unlawful for a corporation, or a separate segregated fund established by a corporation, to solicit contributions to such a fund from any person other than its stockholders and their families and its executives or administrative personnel and their families."[40] Additionally, the law permits a corporation or its PAC to make 2 written solicitations for contributions during the calendar year from any stockholder, executive or administrative personnel, or employee of a corporation or the families of such persons . . . only by mail addressed . . . to their residence and . . . so designed that the corporation . . . cannot determine who makes a contribution of $50 or less as a result of such solicitation and who does not make such a contribution.[41]

FECA also defines executive or administrative personnel to mean "individuals employed by a corporation who are paid on a salary, rather than hourly, basis and who have policymaking, managerial, professional, or supervisory responsibilities."[42] Unsolicited contributions to the PAC, however, may be accepted from any source inside or outside of the corporation[43] with the exception of foreign nationals all of whom are prohibited from making political contributions in the United States.[44]

Critics of corporate PACs claim that these laws cannot safeguard the rights of corporate personnel because the workplace is "the black hole in American rights" in which individuals as employees do not enjoy the same constitutional guarantees they do as citizens.[45] They claim that voluntary participation by employees in the PAC as required by FECA may not be possible because of psychological pressures and incentive systems that remain even in the absence of physical force, job discrimination, and actual or threatened reprisals; all of which have been declared illegal tactics for obtaining donations from employees.[46] Amitai Etzioni states that "hierarchy and truly free consent are difficult to reconcile."[47] The methods used by the corporation or its affiliated PAC to solicit donations for the PAC, therefore, reflect on the corporation as an employer and citizen as well as affect the ability of the PAC to raise money to be used for its political purposes.

Table 6 reveals that among the *Fortune* corporations with PACs, there is an awareness of this hierarchical problem, and many of them have chosen to resolve it, in part, by imposing on themselves a more restrictive solicitation policy than is required by FECA. Most of these companies solicit only senior managers alone or in combination with middle managers and avoid soliciting stockholders, other exempt employees or all employees by mail twice a year.

Companies often do not take full advantage of their solicitation rights because of complex job descriptions or special ranking sys-

Table 6
Solicitation Patterns of *Fortune* Corporate PACs

Solicited Class	No. of Corporations Soliciting	% of Total
Stockholders	13	8.6
Senior Executives	111	73.5
Middle Management	98	65.0
All Exempt Employees*	52	34.4
All Employees (at home)	5	3.3
Total Number of Respondents	151	

Source: Responses from questionnaires.

* Thirteen additional companies noted that some exempt employees were solicited. These companies used a minimum base salary level to determine the group from whom contributions were sought. If these companies are included in the exempt solicitation category, the results would show 65 companies or 43%.

tems that make it difficult to define their management categories to comply with FECA's. The fear of violating the law has prevented them from expanding their solicitation effort further down into salaried ranks. Additionally, some companies are opposed to drawing lines between individuals and creating "an unnatural caste system" which might adversely affect their employee relations without necessarily increasing the contributions to the PAC.[48]

Top managers are solicited most frequently because they have the highest incomes, most responsibility, and most contact with the government and, therefore, are most likely to contribute to the PAC. As one moves down the corporate pyramid into the lower ranks which have more people in them, the solicitation effort is less effective and more costly and thus is often disregarded.[49]

Stockholders also are rarely solicited because they are a large group with widely divergent political views. Mail solicitation, which is expensive for most publicly held corporations, has been largely unsuccessful in obtaining contributions that would make this effort cost-effective. Personal solicitation has been effective but is rarely feasible.[50]

The reluctance of corporate PACs to take full advantage of their solicitation privileges has disturbed their proponents. They believe that all corporate employees should be given the opportunity to participate in the corporate PAC in order to stimulate their political awareness and to avoid an appearance of disenfranchisement.[51] Inasmuch as most people who contribute to a PAC are unlikely to engage in any other form of traditional campaign activity, it is also argued that a broader solicitation policy among corporate PACs would bring more individuals into the political process.[52]

In addition to encouraging participation in democracy, expanded solicitation practices by corporate PACs also may benefit the PAC. According to S. Prakash Sethi,

By broadening PAC membership to include all individuals eligible to join, including the biannual solicitation of employees permitted by the law, the PAC can become a means for developing public policy positions on social issues in line with the public interest as perceived by the corporate constituency as a whole rather than by a few key officers, who may or may not represent their employees or shareholders.[53]

Through a better understanding of the public interest, the corporate PAC should be able to enhance the company's political power, public image, and ultimately its success in shaping public policies affecting the private sector.

Although appealing on the basis of democratic principles, this argument for wider solicitation practices does not take into consideration the diminishing response rate experienced by corporate PACs which have solicited throughout the ranks of their corporation as reflected in table 7. There appears to be an inverse relationship between the size of the group being solicited and the participation rate of that group.[54] Individuals at higher levels within a corporation are more receptive to PAC solicitations. Reaching them is also less complex and less expensive; thus the return on investment made by the corporation in a limited solicitation effort is greater than it would be if more people were solicited.

Greater efforts in developing political education programs, voter registration and get-out-the-vote drives, and internal political communications have aided corporations in heightening awareness, appreciation, and identification with company interests among salaried employees and management in recent years. Nonetheless, this has not necessarily translated into gaining the support of these groups for a corporate PAC at election time because it is likely that "members of the corporation do not, in the same fashion, identify with the political goals of the firm; for shareholders and employees, the

Table 7
Response Rates from Solicited Classes According to *Fortune* Affiliated
Corporate PACs

% of Responses	Number of Companies Reporting Solicited Classes				
	Stockholders	Senior Management	Middle Management	All Exempt	All Employees
0–10	6	4	13	13	1
11–20	1	7	10	10	2
21–30	0	7	13	4	0
31–40	0	4	12	9	1
41–50	2	6	12	7	0
51–60	0	6	8	1	0
61–70	0	3	4	0	0
71–80	0	19	4	1	0
81–90	1	18	3	1	0
91–100	0	20	1	0	0

Source: Responses from questionnaires. The reader should remember that the higher percentage of responses occurs most often in solicited classes which have a small membership; whereas, the lower response rates are found in groups with larger memberships. Therefore, the response rates are relative rather than absolute results.

importance of corporate affiliation is usually secondary to other forms of self-identification."[55] Corporations which would prefer to expand their PAC's solicitation to include a broader corporate constituency might be able to achieve better response rates if they stress bread-and-butter issues such as competition, taxes, or jobs with which employees can identify more closely rather than emphasize philosophical issues such as free enterprise.[56]

Regardless of which group or groups are targeted by the solicitation effort, the success of any fund-raising activity is dependent on the techniques employed in reaching them. Technically, no prohibitions exist regarding the methods that may be used by a corporate PAC for soliciting stockholders and management personnel so long as those who are solicited are not coerced, are assured that their contributions are voluntary, are guaranteed that there will be no reprisals for not contributing, and are told about the political purpose of their contribution. These requirements, which were first spelled out by the FEC in the SUN-PAC Advisory Opinion and are discussed in chapter 2, were accompanied by a recommendation that no superior be permitted to solicit donations from subordinates in order to avoid even the appearance of coercion.

Despite these guidelines, critics of corporate PACs remain convinced that coercion of a subtle or covert nature still occurs. They claim that stockholders are solicited less frequently than employees in all categories because stockholders are less susceptible to coercion and, therefore, are less likely to contribute. These critics emphasize that the restricted, salaried classes that a corporate PAC may solicit on a regular basis are the most vulnerable to internal pressure from peers because of their desire to appear to be team players.[57]

The issue of coercion regarding the solicitation practices of corporate PACs came to a head in 1979 in *International Association of Machinists and Aerospace Workers et al. v. FEC et al.* The union brought suit on the basis that the employer-employee relationship was inherently pregnant with coercive possibilities, particularly for those members of management who were unprotected by contractual or union agreements. Middle managers, in particular, were viewed as vulnerable because they needed their employer's goodwill to be promoted and were unprotected by a shroud of privacy.[58] The Supreme Court's refusal to grant a writ of certiorari has left this issue unresolved for the critics of corporate PACs. They continue to perceive the solicitation process as containing inherently coercive relationships despite all disclaimers to the contrary. Table 8 reflects the solicitation methods being used by 151 of the *Fortune* affiliated corporate PACs. It reveals that group presentations and letters signed by the Chief Executive Officer (CEO) are most frequently used. Newsletters, postal solicitations, and in-person methods also are used by slightly over one-third of these PACs. To what extent any of these methods is coercive cannot be determined by simply addressing the issue of methodology alone because the wording of the letter, the relationship among individuals, the attitude of individuals, and other important variables remain unknown.

To determine the potential for coercion in the solicitation proc-

Table 8
Solicitation Methods Used by *Fortune* Affiliated Corporate PACs

Solicitation Methods	No. of Companies Using Method	% of Total* (Total = 151)
Letter from CEO	82	54
Person to Person	54	36
Group Presentation	92	61
Phone Solicitation	5	3
Postal Solicitation** (Other than CEO letter)	55	36
Newsletter	62	41
Other**	26	17

Source: Responses from questionnaires.

* This column does not total 100 percent because many corporations use several solicitation methods.

** In the Other category, twenty respondents stated that they used a solicitation letter signed by someone other than the CEO such as the PAC chair, government relations officer, general counsel, or treasurer of the PAC. If these responses were added to the Postal Solicitation category, the number of companies using that method of solicitation would rise to seventy five, and they would represent 50 percent of the corporations responding to the questionnaire.

ess, it is also necessary to reflect on the relationship between the solicitor and the solicitee. As shown in table 9, *Fortune* corporate PACs use peers as solicitors most frequently but also call upon specific officers to make a plea for funds either in person, in group sessions, or by mail. The substantial involvement of corporate officials as well as supervisors in the solicitation process adds fuel to the critics' fire regarding potential coercion.

The degree of coercion involved in corporate PAC solicitation also is dependent on the degree of anonymity afforded contributors and those who do not contribute. This is an inverse relationship because the feeling of being coerced experienced by the solicitee is likely to decrease as the security surrounding the identity of contributors to the corporate PAC increases. Because FECA requires that the names of all contributors of $200 or more be filed by the PAC, large contributors cannot retain their privacy.[59] Nonetheless, collection practices can reflect the desire of the corporate PAC to provide most contributors with confidentiality. Table 10

Table 9
Solicitors Used by *Fortune* Affiliated Corporate PACs

Solicitor	No. of Companies Using Solicitor	% of Total* (Total = 151)
Supervisors	30	20
Peers	70	46
Subordinates	28	19
Other**	64	42

Source: Responses from questionnaires.

* This column does not total 100 percent because some companies reported using more than one category of solicitors.

** Among those replying Other, thirty companies named the solicitor for their PAC as the CEO or PAC treasurer, and ten others named the government relations or public affairs officer.

Table 10
Collection Methods Used by *Fortune* Affiliated Corporate PACs

Collection Methods*	No. of Companies Using Method	% of Total** (Total = 151)
Payroll Deduction	113	75
Lump Sum	79	52
Monthly Billing	0	0
Pledge with Delayed Billing	8	5
Other	3	2

Source: Responses from questionnaires.

* This list of collection methods was adapted from Edward Handler and John R. Mulkern, *Business in Politics: Campaign Strategies of Political Action Committees* (Lexington, Mass.: Lexington Books, 1982), p.46.

** This column totals more than 100 percent because some companies used more than one collection method.

reflects the heavy reliance placed by *Fortune* corporate PACs on payroll deduction for collection of their contributions. This method is favored because it is administratively simple and inexpensive and provides the PAC with an accurate estimation of its cash flow.[60] Unfortunately, it also may compromise confidentiality.[61]

An awareness of this problem among the *Fortune* affiliated PACs was evident. They attempted to alleviate the situation through "need to know" or "third party" solutions. "Need to know" approaches limited the number of persons who were made privy to the identity of the PAC's donors. Where this could not be accomplished satisfactorily, companies relied on coded formats, secured computers, or severe penalties such as immediate dismissal to prevent the unnecessary identification of donors or noncontributors.

"Third party" solutions involved record keeping by a professional individual or organization distinct from the corporation such as a private accountant or bank. This arms-length approach to contribution and data collection was the most effective procedure for maintaining maximum security for contributors and noncontributors to the corporate PAC. The reward for the additional expenses incurred for this service was a better image for the corporate PAC and for its connected corporation.

It would be misleading to state that all corporations are concerned with the issue of confidentiality for their PAC donors. One company's response was that they "use prudence but are not hung up on anonymity." Another company revealed that it was concerned that too high a participation rate might appear to be coercive but intended to give a bronze medallion to each PAC member to encourage greater participation. It is not surprising that these two corporations had a high response rate from among those they solicited. Nonetheless, other corporations showing some degree of insensitivity to the appearance of coercion in their PAC's solicitation or collection practices reported extremely low response rates.

Most corporations are sensitive to the criticism that contributions to their affiliated PAC may be fraught with coercion and attempt to overcome this problem by developing solicitation and collection procedures that are low-key and enhance the voluntary nature of the activity as required by FECA. They realize that Americans do not respond favorably to coercion and that they cannot afford to allow their corporate PAC to damage the company by injuring its relations with its employees or with the public.

The growth of the corporate PAC movement, as noted earlier, will be dependent in the future on the enhanced financial strength of those corporate PACs already in existence because corporations currently without PACs are unlikely to establish them. In light of the general reluctance of the PACs affiliated with the nation's largest corporations to take full advantage of their solicitation privileges and their general attempt to maintain a noncoercive atmosphere for those persons from whom they do solicit, the fear of unlimited corporate PAC growth in the future seems unwarranted.

NOTES

1. Edwin M Epstein, "PACs and the Modern Political Process." Paper presented at the Conference on the Impact of the Modern Corporation, Center for Law and Economic Studies, Columbia University School of Law, The Henry Chauncey Conference Center, Princeton, New Jersey, November 12–13, 1983, pp. 5–6.
2. Cantor, *Political Action Committees*, pp. 28–29.
3. *Ibid.*, p. 28.
4. Epstein, *Business and Labor in the American Electoral Process*, p. 8.
5. Bernadette A. Budde, "Business Political Action Committees," in *Parties, Interest Groups and Campaign Finance Laws*, ed. Michael J. Malbin (Washington, D.C.: American Enterprise Institute for Public Policy Research, 1980), p. 10.
6. *Ibid.*, p. 9.
7. Edwin M. Epstein, "The Emergence of Political Action Committees," in *Political Finance*, ed. Herbert E. Alexander, Sage Electoral Studies Yearbook, Vol. 5 (Beverly Hills, Calif.: Sage Publications, 1979), pp. 162–163.
8. Cantor, *Political Action Committees*, pp. 29–31.
9. Epstein, *Business and Labor in the American Electoral Process*, p. 13.
10. Budde, "The Practical Role of Corporate PACs in the Political Process," pp. 559–560.
11. Edwin M. Epstein, "PACs and the Modern Political Process," p. 36. Epstein also points out that using *Fortune* lists is problematic because they do not include all large corporations. They exclude all privately held companies and many large public companies, too (pp. 48–49). To some extent, however, the expansion of the *Fortune* nonindustrial listings reduces his criticisms.
12. See the appendixes for the lists of the *Fortune* corporations included in this study along with information regarding which ones had had one or more PACs by June 30, 1983. In a few instances, corporations reflected as having had a PAC had discontinued their PAC prior to June 30, 1983, but were included in the study because they had participated in earlier elections.

13. *Ibid.*, p. 36.

14. This growth is somewhat deceptive because ten of these firms also appeared on the *Fortune* 500 list in 1983 and, therefore, are double counted. For purposes of this study, they will be included among the *Fortune* 500 largest industrial firms.

15. In fact, seventy-five bank holding companies appearing on the *Fortune* list have a PAC, but because of a merger between two of them, they are counted as a multiple PAC for one firm.

16. Etzioni, *Capital Corruption*, p. 124. Epstein also notes that industry-specific interaction with the federal government as well as company size is a key variable in determining PAC formation and intensity. Within an industry, size remains the key factor, and the formation of a PAC is most likely to occur when the company has operating revenues, sales, or assets exceeding $1 billion. Epstein, "PACs and the Modern Political Process," pp. 45–46.

17. Edwin M. Epstein, *The Corporation in American Politics* (Englewood Cliffs, N.J.: Prentice-Hall, Inc., 1969), p. 100. In another work, Epstein notes that this close relationship to the government occurs not only when the government is a regulator but also when it acts as promoter, purchaser, tax collector, subsidizer, stabilizer, and resource allocator. Epstein, "PACs and the Modern Political Process," p. 38.

18. Epstein, "PACs and the Modern Political Process," p. 54.

19. Epstein, *The Corporation in American Politics*, pp. 129–132.

20. Lee Ann Elliott, "Political Action Committees—Precincts of the '80's," *Arizona Law Review*, 22, no. 2 (1980), pp. 546–548.

21. Herbert E. Alexander, "Political Finance Regulation in International Perspective," in *Parties, Interest Groups and Campaign Finance Laws*, ed. Malbin, p. 350.

22. The latter reason is of particular interest in light of Advisory Opinion 1983–19 which noted that despite prohibitions in 2 U.S.C. §441e (a) & (b), a corporation with foreign ownership can have a PAC if the corporation is "organized under the law of any state within the United States." Foreign nationals, however, are not permitted to contribute to or to participate in activities of these PACs in any way. Federal Election Commission, Advisory Opinion 1983–19, p. 3.

23. Budde, "Business Political Action Committees," p. 13.

24. "Corporate PACs Grow in Number, Influence," *Management Review*, 69 (October 1980), p. 4.

25. Edie Fraser, "The Future for PACs in Business," in *The PAC Handbook: Political Action for Business*, ed. Fraser/Associates (Cambridge, Mass.: Ballinger Publishing Co., 1982), p. 327.

26. Patrick G. Dooher, Esq., "Deductibility of Corporate Political Expenditures—Grassroots Lobbying and PACs," reprint, p. 3.

27. *Ibid.*, p. 5.

28. *Ibid.*, p. 4.

29. David Jacobs, "Economic Concentration and Political Outcomes: Cross-Sectional and Time Series Examinations of Images of the State." Paper presented at the meeting of the Academy of Management, Dallas, August 1983, pp. 6–7.

30. Steven N. Brenner, "Size Influences on Corporate Political Action Proprieties." Paper presented at the meeting of the Academy of Management, Detroit, August 1980, p. 5.

31. Epstein, *The Corporation in American Politics*, p. 144.

32. *Ibid.*, pp. 144–145.

33. Cantor, *Political Action Committees*, pp. 108–109. The absence of any corporation from the lists of the largest PAC sponsors is a clear example of this obscuring effect. Without it, AT&T would have been among the largest PAC sponsors prior to its breakup, and Sears could be among them in the future.

34. Edie Fraser "Forward," in *The PAC Handbook*, ed. Fraser Associates.

35. Rep. Newt Gingrich, "Preface," in *A Nation of Associations: The Origin, Development and Theory of the Political Action Committee*, ed Alfred Balitzer (Washington, D.C.: American Society of Association Executives and the American Medical Political Action Committee, 1981), p. 7.

36. Epstein, "The Business PAC Phenomenon," pp. 38–39.

37. Gary C. Jacobson, "Money in the 1980 and 1982 Congressional Elections," in *Money and Politics in the United States*, ed. Malbin, p. 41.

38. U.S. Federal Election Commission, *Record*, 10, no. 3 (March 1984), p. 12.

39. Alexander, *Financing Politics*, pp. 9–18; and Don R. Kendall, "Corporate PACs: Step-by-Step Formation and Troublefree Operation," *Campaigns and Elections*, 1 (Spring 1980), p. 14. Alexander claims that political campaigns are not particularly or inappropriately expensive if compared with the cost of advertising campaigns for many commercial products. Alexander, *Financing Politics*, p. 19.

40. 2 U.S.C. §441b (b) (4) (A) (i).

41. 2 U.S.C. §441b (b) (4) (B).

42. 2 U.S.C. §441b (b) (7).

43. Curtis C. Sproul, "Corporations and Unions in Federal Politics: A Practical Approach to Federal Election Law Compliance," *Arizona Law Review*, 22, no. 2 (1980), p. 485.

44. Advisory Opinion 1983–19 noted that corporations with foreign ownership could have a PAC if the corporation was "organized under

the law of any state within the United States whose principal place of business is within the United States." Foreign nationals in the corporation, however, could not contribute money to this PAC or exercise any control over it.

45. "Browbeating Employees into Lobbyists," *Business Week*, no. 2627 (March 10, 1980), p. 132.

46. Etzioni, *Capital Corruption*, p. 40.

47. *Ibid.*, p. 41.

48. Kendall, "Corporate PACs: Step-by-Step Formation and Troublefree Operation," p. 19.

49. Alexander, *Financing the 1976 Election*, p. 553.

50. Alexander, *Financing Politics*, p. 83; and Joseph J. Fanelli, "Political Action Committees," *The Corporate Director*, 1, no. 1 (January/February, 1980), p. 16.

51. Budde, "Business Political Action Committees," p. 13.

52. Stuart Rothenberg and Richard R. Roldan, *Business PACs and Ideology: A Study of Contributions in the 1982 Elections* (Washington, D.C.: The Institute for Government and Politics of the Free Congress Research and Education Foundation, 1983), p. 5.

53. Sethi, "Serving the Public Interest," p. 10.

54. Alexander, *Financing the 1976 Election*, p. 553.

55. Epstein, *The Corporation in American Politics*, p. 68.

56. John C. Perham, "Big Year for Company Political Action," *Dun's Review*, 111, no. 3 (March 1978), p. 105.

57. Mayton, "Politics, Money, Coercion and the Problem with Corporate PACs," pp. 383–390. These critics suggest that solicitations by corporate PACs be restricted only to shareholders. The effectiveness of this suggestion, however, was diluted by the FEC's Advisory Opinion 1983–35 which stated that employees who participate in a company's stock option plan may be treated as stockholders for purposes of PAC solicitation efforts as long as they have a vested interest in and direct voting power of the stock and can collect dividends. U.S. Federal Election Commission, *FEC Record*, January 1984, p. 5.

58. Alexander, *Financing the 1980 Election*, p. 74.

59. There are several factors which complicate the task of determining who has donated $200 or more to a PAC despite the filing regulations. Filings are periodic and reflect lump sum amounts. Inasmuch as payroll deductions are often less than $200, donors who exceed this limit on a cumulative basis are not reflected immediately. Additionally, since the 1981–82 election cycle the FEC has provided computer printouts reflecting only those persons who have contributed $500 or more, thereby adding some anonymity to those who donate below that amount because noncomputerized records are difficult to obtain even in person.

60. Perham, "Big Year for Company Political Action," p. 102.

61. Vandegrift suggests a solution to this problem by using payroll deduction only for individuals contributing $200 or more to the corporate PAC because their identity must be disclosed through the filing with the FEC. Vandegrift, "The Corporate Political Action Committee," p. 465.

4

CONTRIBUTIONS: PATTERNS AND PURPOSE

Managers who seek to maximize their access to or influence with members of Congress are confronted with the need to retain credibility, an appearance of good citizenship, and an image of responsible behavior for their company. As noted in chapter 3, many managers have attempted to safeguard their company's reputation by refusing to establish a PAC. For those corporations that have underwritten an affiliated PAC, the contribution decision becomes the vehicle through which they reconcile their political activism and their reputation with the public. Corporate PAC contribution decisions, therefore, reflect the contradictions inherent in corporate political involvement as well as the reluctance of many managers to participate fully in the political process or their inexperience in doing so.

Several paths are available to corporations and corporate PACs for disbursing money related to a federal election campaign. As noted earlier, a corporation can expend treasury funds for non-partisan communications or partisan communications, but then only to a restricted audience of stockholders, executives, administrative personnel, and their families. These expenses are not reported to the FEC unless they exceed $2,000 per election.[1] The corporation also can use general revenues for political education, public affairs, and civic action programs as well as registration and get-out-the-vote drives.[2] These expenditures and the treasury funds used to underwrite establishment, administration, or solicitation for an affiliated PAC are proprietary and thus go unreported. As such, they represent "soft money"—funds which are unlimited, untraceable, and exempt from disclosure while being prohibited from direct use in a federal election campaign.[3] Finally, corporations can give in-kind or nonmonetary contributions such as leaves of absence during which time the employee receives compensation valued up to $5,000 from the corporation while working in a candidate's campaign.[4] Because all of these activities are unpublicized, they are unnoticed and create few public relations problems for managers.

Contributions from corporate PACs, however, represent money or in-kind items with monetary value that are provided directly to a candidate for purposes of supporting him or her in a federal election campaign.[5] Because these contributions are subject to ceiling limitations and must be reported to the FEC, they represent "hard money" and are central to the analysis of corporate PAC involvement in and influence on the federal election process. As noted by BIPAC, "The distribution of contributions is key to understanding the goals of the business community."[6]

An understanding of corporate PAC contributions requires consideration of the varied processes by which the recipients of these contributions are selected. Affiliated PACs, serving as alter egos of their corporations, protect the political interests of their connected companies while keeping their funds separate from those of the companies. Donors to the PAC are served only indirectly as members of the corporate community.

Many corporate PACs are run directly by the company's boards of directors or senior managers who "may decide when, how much, and to whom the solicited funds are to be given."[7] When this occurs, there often is little democracy in the selection process. In many other corporations, the boards of directors or senior managers influence the decisions indirectly by selecting the committee that makes the PAC's contribution decisions. This upper-level management control is defended because CEOs cannot "afford to let corporate political activities alienate potential customers, create interdivisional conflict, or weaken employee morale."[8] By selecting managers to make the PAC's decisions, corporate leadership subscribes to the position that "as a general rule, . . . the political interests of the manager are in harmony with the objectives of his organization."[9] Additionally, centralized decision-making allows the PAC to concentrate on the corporate agenda rather than on the differing individual agendas of employees.[10]

Responses received from 147 *Fortune* affiliated corporate PACs confirmed the dominance of senior management in corporate PAC decisions. In 45 PACs, they alone made the candidate selection decisions; in 28 other PACs, they participated in the decision-making committee; and in 80 others, the policy committee was selected by the president, CEO, senior managers, or the board of directors ordinarily for an indefinite period of time. In several instances, however, the appointments were made for two years or for a period of time conforming to the election cycle.

Despite the inherently undemocratic character of corporate PAC decision-making processes, it is incorrect to assume that no regard is given to the political wishes or views of PAC participants. In one-third of the *Fortune* affiliated corporate PACs, members were permitted to earmark their contributions for specific candidates. Inasmuch as earmarked donations represent an individual's, rather than the PAC's, preference for a candidate, "FECA does not count an earmarked contribution toward the $5,000 limit [placed on the PAC]."[11] Earmarking thus benefits the PAC by enhancing the appearance of democracy and may attract more voluntary contributors. Simultaneously, however, earmarking may adversely affect the PAC by creating additional record keeping and reporting costs and by making its contributions policies appear uncertain. This can occur if the earmarked funds are indistinct from the PAC's own contributions in the public's mind and are targeted for different recipients.[12]

Several *Fortune* corporate PACs also infused democratic procedures into their selection process by allowing members to participate in the candidate selection process, by including middle managers, or by seeking representation from a cross-section of the company's geographic, product, or departmental divisions. Corporate PACs which gain an awareness of members' views provide them with a voice in the candidate selection process and keep them informed of the PAC's contribution decisions, develop successful fund-raising efforts, and avoid antagonizing their employees.

Ironically, very few *Fortune* corporate PACs involved their government relations professionals or Washington representatives in the candidate selection process, thus confirming Malbin's observation that "corporations, even large ones with Washington offices, tend to make their campaign decisions somewhere else."[13] In part this may explain the politically naive or inconsistent contribution strategies followed by many corporate PACs. Handler and Mulkern have noted that Washington representatives add pragmatism to contribution decisions and that public affairs specialists lean to their own political preferences. When political amateurs alone control the PAC's choices, ideology rather than pragmatism may prevail.[14]

Although contribution patterns of corporate PACs reflect considerable diversity, they also display substantial similarity. As a result of federal financing, corporate PACs, along with most other PACs, direct little money to the campaigns of candidates for the presidency.[15] Since passage of FECA (1976), PAC contributions have been less attractive to presidential candidates than those provided by individuals, particularly during the nominating process when group contributions, including those from PACs, are not met by matching public funds.[16] In the postconvention or general election period, this issue is moot because all private contributions, either from groups or individuals, are prohibited for any candidate accepting public funding.[17]

The general reluctance of *Fortune* affiliated corporate PACs to involve themselves in presidential primaries is reflected by prohibitions on these contributions in their bylaws and by their behavior. In 1980, only 132 PACs among the 500 largest industrial firms, 9 PACs among the second 500 largest industrial firms, and 118 PACs among the 500 largest service firms (29 bank holding companies, 13 diversified financials, 15 diversified services, 5 retailers, 5 life insurers, 24 transportation, and 27 utilities) gave to a presidential candidate of either party. In 105 instances, these corporate PACs split their contributions among several presidential candidates in one or both parties rather than contributing to only one candidate.[18]

Because of the restrictions on group contributions in presidential primaries and elections, most PAC money has been contributed to congressional candidates. Since 1974, 70 percent of all PAC money has been contributed to candidates for the House of Representatives. Corporate PACs gave 65 percent of their contributions to House candidates in 1980 and 69 percent to them in 1982.[19] PAC money flows most readily to House candidates because they outnumber Senate candidates[20] and do not have the great personal wealth possessed by many Senate candidates. In addition, contribution ceilings reduce the importance of any group's contributions in more costly Senate races.[21] House races occur more frequently than do those for the Senate, and Senate races are often highly competitive and riskier for the investor.[22]

Senate candidates who do receive corporate PAC contributions, however, are likely to get larger sums than are individual House candidates. BIPAC noted that in the 1980 election, *"Fortune* 500 sponsored PACs contributed nearly three and a half times as much money to the average Senate candidate as they gave to the average House candidate. This held true for Democrats as well as Republicans."[23] This is explained by the length of the Senate term, the expense of Senate races, and the greater individual importance of senators within the context of the size of their chamber.

On a per candidate basis, the preference shown by corporate PACs for individual Senate candidates is seen in the significant impact they have had on the total receipts of these candidates. From 1972 to 1980, all PAC contributions accounted for a greater proportion of the contributions received by House candidates than those received by Senate candidates.[24] The percentage of PAC money donated by corporate PACs, however, was greater for Senate candidates than for House candidates.[25]

The distribution of corporate PAC contributions also varies by candidate status. Table 11 reflects their preference for incumbents rather than challengers or open seat contestants from 1976 through 1984.[26] This pattern, which creates an impression of risk aversion or pragmatism rather than ideological commitment in candidate selections,[27] adheres to the theory of the inherent advantages of incumbency, such as a paid professional staff, name recognition, and the franking privilege.[28]

Because of their perceived financial strength, *Fortune* affiliated corporate PACs are considered a potential threat to incumbents because they can afford the assumption of risks, the establishment of long- rather than short-range political goals, and the inclusion of ideology as well as pragmatism in their selection of candidates.[29]

Table 11
The Percentage of Corporate PAC Contributions Made According to Candidate Status*

Election Year	Candidate Status					
	Incumbent		Challenger		Open Seat	
	Corp. PACs	All PACs	Corp. PACs	All PACs	Corp.PACs	All PACs
1976	72	64	18	20	12	15
1978	59	59	22	22	19	19
1980**	60	63	28	25	12	13
1982***	73	66	13	19	14	15
1984	87	80	4	10	9	11

Source: Joseph E. Cantor, *Political Action Committees: Their Evolution and Growth and Their Implications for the Political System* (Washington, D.C: Congressional Research Service, 1981), pp. 116 and 121 for 1976 and 1978. FEC Press Releases dated March 1981 for 1980; April 29, 1983, for 1982; and October 26, 1984, for 1983–1984 figures, which are for an eighteen-month period and are not final figures.

* Corporations without stock are not included.

** The poor showing of pro-business incumbents in 1978 and a large number of excellent pro-business challengers in 1980 is given as the explanation of this reduced support for incumbents by corporate PACs in the 1978 and 1980 elections. Joseph J. Fanelli, "Political Action Committees," *The Corporate Director*, 1, no. 1 (January/February 1980), p. 18.

*** The increased support for incumbents again in 1982 is the result of the success of pro-business challengers in 1980. Amitai Etzioni, *Capital Corruption* (San Diego: Harcourt Brace Jovanovich, 1984), p. 31. Obviously the current incumbents also must have been viewed as pro-business in light of the early FEC results for 1984.

Table 12, however, shows that *Fortune* affiliated corporate PACs appear to have no greater preference for challengers or for open seat contestants instead of incumbents than do PACs affiliated with smaller corporations. By behaving in a manner similar to the PACs of smaller companies, *Fortune* affiliated corporate PACs substantiate the theory of risk aversion rather than prove to be an exception to it and confirm that the size of a corporation does not necessarily correlate with political courage or assertiveness.

Despite their overwhelming support for incumbents, *Fortune* affiliated corporate PACs claim to be motivated in their candidate selection process by many factors, some of which, as noted in table

Table 12
Fortune Affiliated Corporate PACs Favoring Challengers and Open Seat Candidates Rather Than Incumbents from 1978 to 1982*

Fortune List	Election Year		
	1978	*1980*	*1982*
Largest 500 Industrials	57	65	12
Second 500 Industrials	4	6	4
Bank Holding Companies	5	5	2
Diversified Financials	4	3	2
Diversified Services	8	11	8
Retail Companies	1	3	0
Life Insurance Companies	1	3	1
Transportation Companies	0	2	0
Utilities	6	6	0

Source: Marvin Weinberger and David U. Greevy, compilers, *The PAC Directory: A Complete Guide to Political Action Committees* (Cambridge, Mass.: Ballinger Publishing Co., 1982); and David U. Greevy, Chadwick R. Gore, and Marvin I. Weinberger, eds., *The PAC Directory: Book II The Federal Committees* (Cambridge, Mass.: Ballinger Publishing Co., 1984).

* The *Fortune* affiliated corporate PACs included in this study were those which had receipts or expenditures of at least $5,000 in 1978 and at least $10,000 in 1980 or 1982. Smaller *Fortune* affiliated corporate PACs were not reviewed in detail by the authors of the resource books.

13, are considered more influential than incumbency. The concern shown for a candidate's philosophy toward business and voting record, however, favors incumbents who have a track record available for assessment more than challengers or open seat contestants, especially if they have no prior public record. BIPAC has concluded that "while business PACs seek opportunities to elect members of Congress who are sympathetic to their interests, they demonstrate strong support for those candidates who have a proven record of business support."[30]

Nevertheless, PACs did not favor incumbents blindly even when the candidate's status was of concern to them. Rather they distinguished among them on the basis of seniority and committee assignments. In their early years, corporate PAC contributions flowed

Table 13
Candidate Selection Criteria Used by Corporate PACs Affiliated with *Fortune*
Companies

Criteria	No. of PACs	% of Total (144 = 100%)
Incumbency	90	63
(Committee Assignment)	(77)	(53)
(Seniority)	(31)	(22)
Challenger	68	47
Closeness of Race	87	60
Likelihood of Winning	92	64
Philosophy toward Business	139	97
General Voting Record	122	85
Trade Group Support	99	69
Voting Record on Specific Issues Related to Company or Industry	131	91
Other*	44	31

Source: Responses from questionnaires.
*Among these forty-four responses, twenty-three PACs or 16 percent of the
total noted that they gave consideration to candidates in districts where their
company had a facility.

most readily to incumbents with substantial seniority.[31] That they
no longer do so may be attributed to a greater sophistication by
PACs and to the declining importance of seniority itself in Congress because of deaths, defeats, or retirements of entrenched members. Additionally, the election of many younger individuals with
weaker ties to their party, its leaders, and congressional traditions
which would reduce their own influence has eroded the importance
of seniority.[32] Corporate PACs also have altered their support of
incumbents to favor those who are on influential committees concerned with tax policy, appropriations, or business regulation rather
than those on important committees less directly related to business
issues such as the judiciary or foreign affairs.[33]

These candidate selection strategies cast doubt on the political
astuteness and pragmatism of the *Fortune* affiliated corporate PACs.
By rewarding sympathetic or like-minded incumbents for past be-

havior, either consciously or inadvertently, corporate PACs do not maximize their own influence. Instead they should target uncommitted incumbents who could broaden the PAC's future access.[34] Corporate PACs also prevented themselves from increasing the impact of their contributions in situations where the candidates had the greatest need for funds by failing to consider the closeness of a race. Corporate PACs that wish to enhance their influence should consider providing more funds in open seat contests which are highly competitive and in which no candidate has the advantage of incumbency. Challengers who are philosophically pro-business or uncommitted and who can conduct credible campaigns also should be given greater consideration. In the event that they do not win, their earlier showing may provide the base on which they can build for future success. Additionally, supporting a sure winner or safe incumbent in order to reduce the political risk to a major corporation is unnecessary because a winning candidate cannot ignore a large economic institution regardless of whether or not it supported him or her in the last election. As noted by Epstein, "The needs and the welfare of an important corporate constituent are automatically of concern to a legislator, notwithstanding the fact that the corporation may have opposed his election."[35]

Not contributing continually to safe incumbents also can enhance corporate PACs' public image. While it can be argued that even safe incumbents need contributions to protect themselves from potential challengers, to retain the advantage of name recognition among their constituents in an age of population mobility and shift, and to afford the growing expenses associated with campaigns,[36] there is an appearance of impropriety associated with contributing to entrenched individuals. This problem will increase if incumbents horde their excess funds, use them for personal rather than campaign expenses, or establish personal PACs through which they funnel money to other candidates, some of whom may not be favored by the corporate PAC making the original contribution.[37]

Some companies practice split giving—contributing to more than one candidate in a race in order to resolve the dilemmas of incumbency or a tight contest. Handler and Mulkern claim that this is a response "to conflicting pressures . . . generated by key political contests that assume special importance for the committees and their constituencies."[38] Proponents of this practice believe that it allows all PAC members to provide contributions to candidates they prefer and protects the corporation's access to successful candidates regardless of the outcome of the election. Conversely, however, it dissipates the PAC's unified effort; gives an adverse appearance of corruption, double-dealing, and a lack of integrity; and makes the successful candidate less appreciative of the support he or she received from the PAC. Hedging, therefore, may exaggerate rather than reduce corporate PACs' political and public relations risks. In light of the drawbacks associated with this practice, 102 of the 145 *Fortune* respondents noted that they would not contribute to both sides in the same contest. Several others noted that they rarely did so.

In summary, corporate PACs blend philosophical and pragmatic approaches when contributing to incumbents. The PACs stress criteria other than incumbency in their decision-making but behave in a defensive manner which favors incumbents. This apparent contradiction between theory and practice is explained by the fact that "PACs seldom support candidates whose philosophy is compatible with theirs, if they have no chance to win."[39] Given the inherent advantages of incumbency, it is not surprising that incumbents with proven, pro-business track records are favored by corporate PACs more often than are similarly inclined challengers or open seat contestants. Nonetheless, corporate PACs should give greater consideration to sympathetic challengers in tight races where their funding can be of greater importance because it has been determined that spending by an incumbent cannot necessarily overcome the momentum of a well-funded challenger and that "the more both candidates spend, the better the challenger does."[40]

The risk aversion and defensiveness of corporate PACs also is reflected in the timing of their contributions. Corporate PACs, including 72 percent of the *Fortune* respondents, do not contribute ordinarily during congressional primaries, thus missing the opportunity to influence the nominating stage of the election cycle or to take full advantage of their contribution privileges. Additionally, their contributions frequently are given late in the general election campaign, which has a bandwagon effect in anticipation of the winner.[41] These tactics greatly reduce the political efficacy of corporate PAC contributions in determining the winner of a race and give a negative impression of trying to gain access to office-holders. This is especially true if the money is given to eliminate a postelection campaign debt.[42]

The timing of PAC contributions also may affect candidates in different degrees. Challengers, in particular, need early, up-front money to launch a successful campaign and to overtake an incumbent. Corporate PACs favor incumbents not only by contributing to them more often but also by giving money to challengers too late in their campaigns.[43]

In addition to favoring incumbents through the choice or timing of their contributions, corporate PACs reflect a clear preference for Republican candidates as noted in table 14. The *Fortune* PACs also reflected this preference with the exception of diversified financial companies and life insurance companies in 1978 and transportation companies in 1978, 1980, and 1982. There was, however,

Table 14
Partisan Preferences of Corporate PACs* and All PACs

Election Year			Party			
					*Other****	
	Republican		*Democrat*			
	Corp.	All	Corp.	All	Corp.	All
			(Expressed in Percentages)			
1976	57	34	43	66	0	0
1978	66	46	34	54	0	0
1980	62	46	38	54	0	0
1982	66	46	34	54	0	0
1984	54	61	46	39	0	0

Source: Cantor, *Political Action Committees*, pp. 116 and 121 for 1976 and 1978. FEC Press Releases of March 1981 for 1980 data; April 29, 1983, for 1982 data; and October 26, 1984, for 1984 data. The 1984 data is for the first eighteen months of the 1983-84 election cycle.

* Corporations without stock are omitted. The figures include only those contributions made to candidates actually running for office in the appropriate election cycle.

** While corporate PACs as well as all other PACs show a preference for one of the major parties, these results definitely reflect that PACs of all types support the two-party system.

no total uniformity in partisan preference as shown in table 15. Although the corporate PAC community gave twice as much money to Republicans than to Democrats between 1976 and 1980,[44] it is not monolithic on partisan issues. Corporate PACs cannot afford to be purely partisan in their candidate selection because business must address a multiplicity of issues and concerns for facilities located in many different districts, some of which may be represented by Democrats.[45]

Corporate PACs should consider more contributions to Democrats, including those of liberal persuasion who have rarely received corporate PAC contributions in the past. Liberal Democrats have shown a concern for jobs and wages which could on occasion make them natural allies for business on issues related to tariffs and trade barriers.[46] Additionally, Democrats may be less likely to reduce favors to business in order to assist non-elites and "are more likely to give tax breaks to industry."[47] More corporate PAC funding for Democrats also could reduce their dependence on labor

Table 15
Fortune Affiliated Corporate PACs Which Contributed More Often to Democrats or Which Gave Democrats a Higher Average Contribution

Fortune List	More Democrats			Higher Average $		
	1978	*1980*	*1982*	*1978*	*1980*	*1982*
Largest 500 Industrials	46	47	37	48	47	43
Second 500 Industrials	1	10	11	2	11	14
Bank Holding Companies	20	23	27	15	23	26
Diversified Financial	9	10	15	8	15	12
Diversified Services	7	9	12	6	13	12
Retail Companies	3	6	4	3	6	5
Life Insurance	2	7	7	3	7	11
Transportation	17	20	16	18	21	20
Utilities	15	20	14	14	18	18
Total	121	152	143	117	161	161

Source: U.S. Federal Election Commission, "D" Indices for the election cycles of 1977-78, 1979-80, and 1981-82. Computer printouts.

and provide them with the financial freedom to pursue policies that might be more favorable to business.[48]

The hesitancy of corporate PACs to become dominant players in the financing of federal election campaigns is obvious when one reflects on the amounts of money they contribute to individual candidates. Although some corporate PACs are able to raise considerable sums for distribution in election campaigns, most corporate PACs are not very large and do not contribute great amounts of money. According to a study made by the Public Affairs Council regarding the election cycle of 1981–82, the average aggregate contributions made by all corporate PACs registered with the FEC was $18,590. This figure rose to $22,103 when only active corporate PACs which participated in the election were included.[49] According to the FEC's figures for the first eighteen months of the 1983–84 election cycle, no corporate PACs appeared on the lists of the top fifty money raisers or spenders while four corporate PACs affiliated with Lockheed, Philip Morris, Rockwell International, and Amoco (Standard Oil of Indiana) were among the top fifty contributors to federal candidates.[50] As noted in table 16, the average aggregate contribution differs among the *Fortune* PACs. It is greater among the largest 500, diversified services, retail, transportation, and utility companies than it is for all active corporate

Table 16
Average Aggregate Contributions Made by *Fortune* Affiliated Corporate PACs

Election Year	Largest 500	Second 500	Bank Holding Companies	Diversified Financials
1978	$22,635	$3,736	$4,318	$14,038
1980	34,094	4,522	8,029	14,380
1982	41,466	5,055	11,180	22,533

	Diversified Services	Retail	Life Insurance	Transportation	Utilities
1978	$14,893	$24,713	$11,880	$21,424	$11,082
1980	25,470	43,720	9,863	30,482	20,950
1982	31,297	43,119	20,642	33,399	24,730

Source: FEC "D" Indices. Computer printouts.

Table 17
Distribution of Contributions from *Fortune* Affiliated Corporate PACs
by Dollar Amount

Election Year	0–$100	$101–$250	$251–$500	$501–$750
1978	3,560	5,222	6,194	809
1980	2,886	9,235	10,410	1,605
1982	1,195	10,821	12,195	2,165
	$751–$1,000	$1,001–$1,500	$1,501–$2,500	
1978	1,548	407	330	
1980	3,490	1,023	930	
1982	4,814	1,574	1,401	
	$2,501–$5,000	$5,000 +		
1978	155	32		
1980	536	78		
1982	680	160		

Source: FEC "D" Indices. Computer printouts.

PACs. Average aggregate contributions by the second 500, bank holding companies, and life insurance companies are smaller than are those made by all active corporate PACs. Diversified financial service companies are the only ones which approximate the average for all active corporate PACs.

A review of the average contribution made per candidate also reveals that corporate PACs prefer to contribute small amounts to many candidates rather than large amounts to a few candidates. According to the Public Affairs Council, the average corporate PAC contribution to a single federal candidate in 1981–82 was $657.[51] This was lower than the contribution ceilings set by FECA for either individuals ($1,000) or for multicandidate committees ($5,000).[52] Among the *Fortune* affiliated corporate PACs, the same preference can be seen in table 17. Although the size of each contribution made to a federal candidate by a *Fortune* corporate PAC generally has risen with each election cycle, the tendency to provide more candidates with small sums persists. Those who would reduce the contribution ceilings in order to reduce the financial influence of corporate PACs, therefore, are unlikely to achieve their goal because lower contribution ceilings would leave most corporate PACs, including those affiliated with the nation's largest companies, unaffected. If these "reforms," however, encourage greater collaboration among business PACs or greater reliance on independent expenditures (discussed in chapters 5 and 6, respectively), then they would be more detrimental than beneficial to the political system or to the corporate PACs themselves.

The influence of corporate PACs, therefore, is not derived from their individual financial strength but rather from their substantial number and their potential for collective action. This threat is alleviated by the heterogeneity of the business community and the diversity of interests displayed even within the same industry. Corporate PACs do not concentrate their contributions to the same extent as have labor PACs or unaffiliated ideological ones.[53]

Despite these findings, critics of corporate PACs remain concerned that the corporate community will have undue financial influence in federal elections and, ultimately, over national affairs. They support their position by studying congressional voting patterns on controversial pieces of legislation or on issues of importance to a particular industry and seek to correlate the behavior of members of Congress with the preferences of the corporate PACs which contributed to their election campaigns. Several studies cast doubt on these attempts to prove causal relationships[54] because they frequently seek to prove preestablished opinions rather than test a broad spectrum of congressional voting behavior. They also rarely consider the money spent in opposition to the corporate PACs or the likelihood that the same outcome would have occurred in the absence of corporate PAC funding because of a predisposition of the members of Congress on the issue. Although there may be a causal relationship between contributions and the voting behavior of members of Congress, this causality is unclear and may occur in both directions.[55]

Additionally, it has been noted that "the effects of PAC spending is small" when compared to other kinds of influences on congressional voting such as ideology, party, and constituency.[56] In particular, the constituency factor should not be overlooked because, in the last analysis, members of Congress are elected by their constituents and not by PACs. Candidates cannot afford to alienate constituents or to accept funds from any contributor held in low esteem by the public.[57] Successful corporate PACs, therefore, are not only financially strong but also aware of their public relations. PAC decision-makers establish noncontroversial policies for distribution of contributions in order to prevent the alienation of their corporate constituency as well as the constituency of the candidates they support. Corporate PACs are kept bipartisan even though they may favor one party, are restrained from involvement in divisive primaries, and avoid entering races too early before a candidate's chances are known. While not bold political strategies, these policies alienate few people and reduce the controversy confronting the PAC or its connecting corporation[58] and reflect the decision of most corporate PACs to be more concerned with their public image than their political effectiveness.

NOTES

1. In 1975–76 four corporations had to report communications expenses. In 1980 only one firm, Mesa Petroleum, was required to report these expenses, Alexander, *Financing the 1980 Election*, p. 416.

2. Joseph J. Fanelli, "PAC Overview," in *The PAC Handbook*, ed. Fraser/Associates, pp. 21–23.

3. Elizabeth Drew, *Politics and Money* (New York: Macmillan Publishing Co., 1983), pp. 99, 111.

4. Perham, "The New Zest of the Corporate PACs," p. 51.

5. H. Richard Mayberry, Esq., "Business Political Action Committees: A Significant Factor in 1980 Election Results," in *The PAC Handbook*, ed. Fraser/Associates, p. 348.

6. BIPAC, "Distribution of Contributions—The Candidate Perspective: Part Two of the *Fortune* 500 PACs and the 1980 Congressional Elections," *Politikit* (December 1981), p. 21. (Reprint)

7. Vandegrift, "The Corporate Political Action Committee," p. 459.

8. Michael J. Malbin, "Looking Back at the Future of Campaign Finance Reform: Interest Groups and American Elections," in *Money and Politics in the United States*, ed. Malbin, p. 259.

9. Epstein, *The Corporation in American Politics*, p. 13. Not all observers are in total agreement on this point. Some believe that "individual motives and attitudes of corporate officers are crucial in determining both the degree of political involvement and the form it takes." Gary C.

Jacobson, *Money in Congressional Elections* (New Haven: Yale University Press, 1980), p. 83.

10. In an article in the *Harvard Business Review*, one author claimed that 80 percent of the respondents to his survey said that corporate political positions reflected management views only, and 70 percent said that corporate political interests are not democratically determined. Steven N. Brenner, "Business and Politics—An Update," *Harvard Business Review*, 57, no. 6 (November/December 1979), p. 151.

11. BIPAC, "Business Activity in the 1980 Election: A Study of PACs Sponsored by *Fortune* 500 Companies," *Politikit* (November 1981), p. 36. (Reprint)

12. Handler and Mulkern, *Business in Politics*, pp. 79, 82.

13. Michael J. Malbin, "Campaign Financing and the Special Interests," *The Public Interest*, no. 56 (Summer 1979), p. 34.

14. Handler and Mulkern, *Business in Politics*, pp. 27, 69.

15. Less than 4 percent of all PAC money went to presidential contenders in the 1980 election cycle. Cantor, *Political Action Committees*, p. 65

16. Rhodes Cook, "Fund Raising Doubles Since Four Years Ago," *Congressional Quarterly Weekly Report*, 38, no. 8 (February 23, 1980), p. 571.

17. Perham, "The New Zest of the Corporate PACs," p. 50.

18. The 605 contributions made by *Fortune* corporate PACs to presidential contestants in 1980 were distributed on a partisan basis with 416 going to Republicans, 154 to Democrats, and 35 to independents.

19. FEC Press Releases, March 1981 and April 29, 1983.

20. Epstein, "PACs and the Modern Political Process," p. 25.

21. Conway, "PACs, the New Politics, and Congressional Campaigns," in *Interest Group Politics*, ed. Allan J. Cigler and Burdette A. Loomis, p. 131.

22. *Ibid.*

23. BIPAC, "Distribution of Contributions—The Candidate Perspective," p. 21.

24. Cantor, *Political Action Committees*, pp. 75, 78.

25. FEC Press Releases, March 1981 and April 29, 1983.

26. The preference for incumbents is not unique to corporate PACs. With the exception of unaffiliated, ideological PACs, all PACs prefer incumbents, and many do so to a greater degree than do corporate PACs. Cantor, *Political Action Committees*, p. 171.

27. John Holcomb, "Contribution Strategies of Business PACs: Industry and Regional Variations" (Paper presented at the meeting of the American Political Science Association, Washington, D.C., August 30–September 2, 1984), p. 7; and Mayton, "Politics, Money, Coercion and

the Problem with Corporate PACs," p. 381. Not everyone considers corporate PACs more pragmatic than ideological in their candidate selection. In one study the author makes a case for the ideological motivation of corporate PACs' selections of candidates to support. Rothenberg, *Campaign Regulation and Public Policy*, pp. 38–40.

28. Jonathan Walters, "PACs: Do They Buy Votes or Support a Point of View?" *Association Management*, 35 (July 1, 1983), p. 56. In an interesting article which approaches this issue from the vantage point of microeconomic theories of supply and demand, Silberman and Yochum conclude that the behavior of corporate PACs toward incumbents is economically rational, especially when first-and second-term incumbents are supported over challengers and long-term incumbents. Jonathan Silberman and Gilbert Yochum, "The Market for Special Interest Campaign Funds: An Exploratory Approach," *Public Choice*, 35, no. 1 (1980), pp. 75–83.

29. Holcomb, "Contribution Strategies of Business PACs, " pp. 7–8. Malbin believes that risks are more likely to be taken by younger corporate PACs rather than older, larger ones. Michael J. Malbin, "The Business PAC Phenomenon: Neither a Mountain Nor a Molehill," *Regulation*, 3, no. 3 (May/June 1979), p. 43. Epstein also considers larger PACs to be more pragmatic and likely to favor incumbents. Epstein, "PACs and the Modern Political Process," p. 83.

30. BIPAC, "Distribution of Contributions—The Candidate Perspective," p. 27.

31. Perham, "Big Year for Company Political Action," p. 100.

32. Epstein, "PACs and the Modern Political Process," p. 67.

33. Drew, *Politics and Money*, p. 67.

34. Theodore J. Eismeier and Philip H. Pollock III, "Political Action Committees: Varieties of Organization and Strategy," in *Money and Politics in the United States*; ed. Malbin, p. 123.

35. Epstein, *The Corporation in American Politics*, p. 198.

36. Drew, *Politics and Money*, pp. 68–69; and Malbin, ed., *Parties, Interest Groups and Campaign Finance Laws*, pp. 194–197.

37. Of the 144 *Fortune* affiliated corporate PACs responding to an inquiry regarding their willingness to contribute to safe incumbents, 70 said they would, and 74 said they would refuse.

38. Handler and Mulkern, *Business in Politics*, p. 84.

39. Elliott, "Political Action Committees—Precincts of the '80's," p. 552.

40. Gary C. Jacobson, "The Effects of Campaign Spending on Congressional Elections," *The American Political Science Review*, 72, no. 2 (June 1978), p. 470. Some concern has been raised that the emphasis placed by corporate PACs on incumbents and pro-business candidates

could adversely affect the ability of female candidates, who are most frequently challengers and often without business experience, to attract contributions from corporate PACs. A recent study, however, has shown that female candidates raise money in approximately the same manner as do male candidates and that they received one-third of their contributions from PACs. Barbara C. Burrell, "Women's and Men's Campaigns for the U.S. House of Representatives, 1972–1982: A Finance Gap?" Paper presented at the meeting of the American Political Science Association, Washington, D.C., September 1984, p. 11. Additionally, David U. Greevy et al., eds. *The PAC Directory: Book I, The Federal Candidates* (Cambridge, Mass.: Ballinger Publishing Company, 1984), pp. 18–639, identified corporate PACs as contributors to 45 of the 105 female candidates for Congress in 1982. The pattern followed by corporate PACs in these contributions closely paralleled the traits discussed in this section based on incumbency and partisan preference.

41. Epstein, *Business and Labor in the American Electoral Process*, pp. 64, 66. Malbin and Skladony illustrate this phenomenon for the three federal elections from 1978 to 1982. In all instances, incumbents received a larger proportion of early money than did nonincumbents. Michael J. Malbin and Thomas W. Skladony, "Appendix: Selected Campaign Finance Data, 1974–82," in *Money and Politics in the United States*, ed. Malbin, pp. 308–310.

42. Etzioni, *Capital Corruption*, p. 42.

43. David W. Adamany, "PACs and the Democratic Financing of Politics," *Arizona Law Review*, 22, no. 2 (1980), p. 591.

44. Epstein, "PACs and the Modern Political Process," p. 64.

45. Budde, "Business Political Action Committees," in *Parties, Interest Groups, and Campaign Finance Laws*, ed. Malbin, p. 17.

46. Handler and Mulkern, *Business in Politics*, p. 12.

47. Jacobs, "Economic Concentration and Political Outcomes," p. 18.

48. Jacobson, "Money in the 1980 and 1982 Congressional Elections," in *Money and Politics in the United States: Financing Politics in the 1980s*, ed. Malbin, pp. 44–45. Sabato claims that this occurred in 1982 when many Democrats adjusted their positions to a pro-business posture and attracted additional corporate PAC funds. Larry J. Sabato, *Pac Power* (New York: W. W. Norton and Co., 1984), p. 91.

49. Information provided by Richard Anderson of the Public Affairs Council during a panel discussion on August 31, 1984, at the annual meeting of the American Political Science Association in Washington, D.C.

50. FEC Press Release, October 26, 1984, pp. 5–7.

51. Information provided by Richard Anderson.

52. The former ceiling applies to separate, segregated funds which do

not qualify for multicandidate status. In 1981/82, 116 *Fortune* affiliated corporate PACs, 17 percent of the total, did not qualify for multicandidate status.

53. Malbin, "Campaign Financing and the Special Interests," p. 29.

54. Epstein, "PACs and the Modern Political Process," p. 116.

55. Janet Grenzke, "Campaign Financing Practices and the Nature of Representation." Paper presented at the meeting of the American Political Science Association, Washington, D.C., August 30–September 2, 1984, p. 3.

56. Eismeier and Pollock, "Political Action Committees," in *Money and Politics in the United States*, ed. Malbin p. 123; and Henry W. Chappell, Jr., "Campaign Contributions and Congressional Voting: A Simultaneous Probit-Tobit Model," *The Review of Economics and Statistics*, 64, no. 1 (February 1982), p. 83.

57. Michael Johnston, *Political Corruption and Public Policy in America* (Monterey, Calif.: Brooks/Cole Publishing Co., 1982), p. 160.

58. Budde, "Business Political Action Committees," in *Parties, Interest Groups, and Campaign Finance Laws*, ed. Malbin, p. 21.

5

INTERPAC RELATIONS

Corporate PACs are distinct and separate entities by virtue of their different corporate affiliations. They are capable, nonetheless, of working in concert with each other and with trade associations and unaffiliated PACs that show similar views in order to expand the financial clout of the business community or to enhance the power of an ideological position. To what extent they have chosen to do this is a matter of dispute.

The data in chapter 4 revealed the dominance of certain contribution patterns among corporate PACs, particularly within the same industry. It also reflected considerable diversity related, but not limited, to the factors of size, the nature of the business, the philosophy of management, and the organization and operation of corporations and their affiliated PAC, thus also symbolizing the heterogeneity of the American business community. The issue of collaboration is thus unresolved by simply analyzing the candidate contribution patterns of the corporate PACs.

There persists, however, substantial belief in the existence of coordination and collaboration among corporate PACs despite their separate staffs, lack of intertwined control, and distinct funding sources. Many observers contend that similarities in contribution patterns are not simply coincidental and logical outcomes of decisions made by persons with similar beliefs and goals responding in like manner to the same set of stimuli. Rather they believe these are the result of consultation or prearrangement among these persons. This interPAC collusion in the selection of candidates to whom contributions are given is believed to be guided also by centralized trade association PACs which span an industry or industries.[1]

The largest and most influential of these trade association PACs represent a cross-section of the business community and have as members smaller firms which for any of a variety of reasons are unable or unwilling to establish their own PACs.[2] Included within this category are the Business-Industry PAC (BIPAC)[3] and the National Chamber Alliance for Politics, an arm of the Chamber of Commerce of the United States. BIPAC provides information regarding open seat contests and challengers with a pro-business orientation and supplies some funding for friendly incumbents facing difficult opponents.[4] The National Chamber Alliance for Politics provides candidates only with in-kind contributions rather than monetary ones and assists Republican candidates in targeted races where only one candidate is supportive of business and where financial assistance can affect the outcome. Through the publication of their research, analysis, and contribution recommendations, these two national PACs educate and signal the business community regarding their choices of candidates who will make "Congress oriented toward fiscal responsibility, reduction of the federal bureaucracy and support of private enterprise."[5] Their strategies are undoubtedly influential in guiding the PACs of some corporations which do not wish to devote resources to extensive candidate research. The extent of this influence, however, is impossible to ascertain.

Several other national trade association PACs exchange information with and provide guidance for the corporate community and its PACs. Among these are the National Association of Business PACs (NABPAC) which advises 225 member PACs on a variety of PAC-related topics but does not make direct candidate recommendations; the National Association of Manufacturers (NAM) which publishes a monthly newsletter entitled, *The PAC Manager: Decision-Making Information for PAC Administrators;* the National Federation of Independent Business; the Congressional Small Business Campaign Committee; and the National Association for Association PACs (NAFPAC) which assists trade association PACs, many of which are business-related.[6]

Networking among corporate PACs and between them and trade association PACs in their industry does exist but can be used successfully only infrequently and when no organized opposition is present.[7] Trade association PACs play a key role as clearinghouses for information rather than as coordinators of contributions. It is likely, however, that the large national trade association PACs are most influential among the smaller member firms that they service. Inasmuch as these firms often do not have their own PACs this influence does not represent duplicative or coordinated campaign contributions by the business community.

Many political and economic reasons also exist for individual corporate PACs, especially within highly competitive industries, to refuse to adopt political positions established by their trade association's PAC. Among these are the following:

1. The focus of the corporation may be narrower than that of the trade association, and the corporate PAC may have funds to research candidates' positions' and contribute to those sympathetic to its views.

2. Special contracts, licenses, subsidies, and franchises may differentiate firms even within the same industry and create a different outlook and set of goals for a firm as opposed to the industry as a whole.

3. Larger firms are often more concerned with short-term, specific issues; whereas trade associations frequently concentrate on long-term or broader ones.

4. Trade associations may be considered too skewed in partisan leanings, negative, ideological, or ineffectual.[8]

Responses to questionnaires received from 146 corporate PACs on the *Fortune* lists indicated that the influence of trade associations in their candidate selections for purposes of campaign contributions was minimal. Forty-seven of the respondents failed to include trade associations as having any influence in their decisions whatsoever. Those 99 companies which did acknowledge the influence of a trade association on their choice of candidates to support ranked this influence in the manner shown in table 18.

PACs affiliated with the nation's largest companies vary widely regarding their reliance on advice from trade association PACs. As Herbert Alexander has stated, "Because each PAC decides individually which candidates to support, the degree of coordination falls short of the centralized character of business federations in

Table 18
The Degree of Influence that Trade Association PACs Exert on Contribution
Decisions Made by Corporate PACs on the *Fortune* Lists

Degree of Influence	Number of Respondents
1 (Most)	2
2	7
3	13
4	26
5	16
6	10
7	7
8	6
9 (Least)	10
Unranked	2
Total	99

Source: Responses from questionnaires.

foreign countries."[9] Trade associations may attempt to coordinate corporate PAC responses, but they do not dominate them, particularly among the larger corporations. These PACs are often capable of doing and prefer to do their own information gathering and candidate assessments. While the sources of their information may be similar to each other or to those of trade association PACs, their decisions are made separately and often uniquely.[10]

Influence and guidance alone, however, do not fully explain the ties that can exist between a trade association PAC and corporate PACs within the same industry. Trade association PACs are permitted to solicit from among the stockholders, executives, and administrative personnel of a company and their families on an unlimited basis if written permission is granted by the company in advance of the solicitation (2 U.S.C.§441b (4) (D) and 11 C.F.R.§114.8). Theoretically, therefore, the select group of corporate PAC contributors is able to use donations to a trade association PAC supportive of their company as a conduit for funneling duplicate monies to the candidates of their choice. This could lead to a form of vertical proliferation flying in the face of the intent, if not the language, of FECA (1976).[11] In practice, this technique is rarely used.

The rules governing the corporate solicitation activities of trade associations specifically restrict both the trade association and the corporation. The latter may permit only one trade association to solicit the specified groups within the corporation in a calendar year. Trade associations receiving this prior, annual, and specific written permission are limited in their solicitation to the targeted group of stockholders, executives, and administrators and their families and may not seek donations from any other corporate employees. Additionally, the corporation granting the permission may restrict the trade association further by limiting the number of solicitations that it may conduct.[12]

Rather than creating an opportunity for contribution duplications, the rules governing solicitation by trade association PACs within corporations have proven to be too restrictive to be useful. Ironically, this may have stimulated the trade associations' role, discussed above, as a guide for corporate PACs. Bernadette Budde of BIPAC states, "The role of trade associations may be that of encouraging PAC formation among member companies and providing tools and assistance in PAC operation, rather than that of raising large contributions."[13] She contends that these restrictions are inherently discriminatory and are intended to affect trade association PACs adversely. The tendency for trade associations and their PACs to be large only when associated with small companies or entrepreneurial members, which do not have a PAC or where contributions are more easily solicited from the select groups, also is attributed by her to these rules.[14] Regardless of whether or not these correlations are accurate, there is no doubt that trade associations and their PACs are more successful with smaller companies for which they can provide a service and fill a void politically.

Larger firms, particularly those with their own PAC, are not attracted to the double solicitation made by trade associations for a variety of reasons including a desire to avoid competition for donations to their own affiliated PAC, the appearance of preferential solicitation treatment to only one of the many trade associations with which they deal, and, finally, angering the targeted groups which would be solicited twice.[15]

Additionally, trade associations themselves may not seek to solicit within member companies, especially larger ones. Doing so may prove more troublesome than valuable because they are prohibited from using payroll deduction or checkoff methods in the companies and thus are relegated to using less efficient collection methods. Although the companies are able to give the trade association PAC incidental assistance in its solicitation within the company, such as allowing them to use the internal mail system for distribution without requiring reimbursement,[16] there is no guarantee that this aid will be forthcoming, especially if the company has its own PAC.

There is substantial evidence that the large *Fortune* firms do not support the solicitation by trade associations among their stockholders and executives. Of the 147 corporations with PACs responding to an inquiry on this issue, only 12 companies indicated that they permitted this activity while 135 did not. This was true even when the trade association PAC that would have been designated was highly identified within the industry such as BANK-PAC, the trade association PAC established by the American Bankers Association. At the national level, BANKPAC has left the direct solicitation of funds from banking personnel strictly to the individual banks.[17]

It appears that the fear of double solicitation by trade association PACs and the PACs of member companies is unwarranted. Trade associations continue to target portions of the business community that do not have PACs and to have little success in gaining a foothold in major corporations, particularly those with their own PACs. It may be argued, therefore, that trade association PACs primarily supplement corporate PACs by representing otherwise unrepresented business sectors in the financing of federal election campaigns rather than duplicate corporate PAC activity.

InterPAC relations within the business community also can be viewed from the standpoint of funds transferred between PACs. Multicandidate political committees may contribute up to $5,000 in the aggregate to any other political committee including another PAC (2 U.S.C. §441a (a) (2) (C)). It is possible, therefore, for corporate stockholders and executives to funnel money on a personal basis into a trade association PAC to add emphasis to their support for particular candidates or policies and also for corporations with PACs to double their support for candidates or policies through a transfer of funds to a like-minded trade assocation PAC which will contribute it in a similar manner.

Although a trade association PAC cannot solicit corporate PACs for the transfer of funds to their coffers, there is evidence to show that corporate PACs in the largest *Fortune* companies may be mixed in their attitude toward this activity. Of 144 *Fortune* companies with PACs responding to a question regarding their attitude on this issue, 67 companies said that they would consider transferring funds to another PAC while 77 said they would not. It was not clear, however, that those favoring this transfer specifically included trade association PACs among the recipients of these transfers. Their responses were correlated closely to whether they had a state PAC as well as a federal one; therefore, some of those supporting the interPAC transfer of funds may have interpreted the question to mean the transfer of monies between their affiliated PAC at the federal level and another affiliated PAC at the state level or vice versa. Corporate PAC managers interviewed preferred to contribute directly to candidates in order to gain recognition and access for their own company.

Although corporate PAC attitudes are divided on the issue of fund transfers, their actions in this regard are more consistent. Records of the FEC provide clear evidence that fund transfers do not occur often between corporate PACs and major trade association PACs or large unaffiliated PACs with strong conservative, pro-business, or ideological positions. As in other interPAC relations, corporate PACs appear to be reluctant to take advantage of loopholes in the law for bypassing FECA's contribution ceilings but instead act in a responsible manner which does not maximize their financial strength in federal election campaigns. Table 19 reflects the number of PACs affiliated with the *Fortune* corporations which donated funds to nine of the largest trade association or unaffiliated PACs in the 1980 and 1982 election cycles.

To what extent the reluctance of corporate PAC decision-makers to transfer funds to trade association and ideological PACs will continue is uncertain. Of future interest will be their willingness to transfer funds to the personal PACs being established by members of Congress for funneling contributions to their congressional colleagues, thereby gaining additional influence for themselves.[18] The propriety of a corporate PAC making a contribution to the

Table 19
InterPAC Contributions Made by PACs Affiliated with Corporations on the
Fortune Lists to Selected Trade Association and Unaffiliated PACs

Recipient PACs	*Fortune* Donor PACs	
	1980	1982
BIPAC	55	72
National Chamber Alliance for Politics	8	3**
National Conservative PAC (NCPAC)	1	0
BANKPAC	16	20
Committee for the Survival of a Free Congress	1	0
U.S. League of Savings Associations	4	3
National Congressional Club	19*	7***
National Association of Homebuilders	1	0
Fund for a Conservative Majority	1	0

Source:Federal Election Commission, Computer printouts of the "G" Index for the
nine recipient PACs.
* Five of these PACs were affiliated with only two companies, thus the number of
corporations represented as donors was sixteen.
** One of these contributors had received an equal amount from the National
Chamber Alliance, thus the net contribution was zero in dollars.
*** Two of these PACs were affiliated with one corporation, thus the number of
corporations represented as donors was six.

campaign of a member of Congress and then making a second,
separately limited contribution to the private PAC of that member
is suspect and is likely to be avoided by corporate PAC policy
committees concerned about the public appearance of their company. This would be consistent with their other interPAC activities
which have avoided taking political advantage at the expense of
the corporation's reputation.

NOTES

1. Holcomb, "Contribution Strategies of Business PACs, " p. 15; or
Etzioni, *Capital Corruption*, p. 55; or Thomas Byrne Edsall, *The New
Politics of Inequality* (New York: W. W. Norton and Co., 1984), p. 132.
2. U. S. Congress, House, Committee on House Administration, *An*

Analysis of the Impact of the Federal Election Act 1972–78, Institute of Politics, John F. Kennedy School of Government, Harvard University, 96th Cong., 1st sess. (Washington, D.C.: U. S. Government Printing Office, 1979), p. 104.

3. Technically, BIPAC is an independent or unaffiliated PAC rather than a trade association PAC. Nonetheless, its activities closely resemble the latter group more than the former. Budde, "Business Political Action Committees," in Malbin, ed., *Parties, Interest Groups and Campaign Finance Laws*, p. 15.

4. Keith W. Bennett, "PACs: Staying Afloat on the Washington Scene," *Iron Age* (July 2, 1979), p. 36.

5. Joseph J. Fanelli, "PAC Overview" in *The PAC Handbook*, ed. Fraser/Associates, p. 25.

6. Drew, *Politics and Money*, p. 35; and "Will Growth in Numbers Dilute Political Action Committee Effectiveness?"*Cashflow Magazine*, 4, no. 1 (January/February 1983), pp. 20, 22; and Alexander, *Financing the 1980 Election*, p. 375.

7. Edsall, *The New Politics of Inequality*, p. 254 n. 25.

8. Epstein, *The Corporation in American Politics*, pp. 51–53.

9. Alexander, "Political Finance Regulation in International Perspective," p. 350.

10. PACs have several ways in which they can conduct their own research in the candidate selection process before contributing money. They can check voting records on incumbents, review "PAC kits" sent by the candidates, ask candidates to respond to a series of questions, and gather information from their government relations personnel. "Spending Smarter on Political Candidates," *Business Week*, no. 2661 (November 3, 1980), p. 42.

11. John Egan, "Affiliation of Political Action Committees under the Antiproliferation Amendments to the Federal Election Campaign Act of 1971," *Catholic University Law Review*, 29 (Spring 1980), pp. 714, 715, 730.

12. Thomas J. Schwarz and Alan G. Straus, "The Trade Association," in *The Corporation in Politics 1980*, ed. Schwarz and Nielsen, pp. 191–197.

13. Budde, "Business Political Action Committees," in Malbin, ed., *Parties, Interest Groups, and Campaign Finance Laws*, p. 14.

14. Budde, "The Practical Role of Corporate PACs in the Political Process," p. 561.

15. Kendall, "Corporate PACs: Step-by-Step Formation and Troublefree Operation," p. 19.

16. Schwarz and Straus, "The Trade Association," in *The Corporation in Politics 1980*, ed. Schwarz and Nielsen, p. 198.

17. "Bankers' Political Action Committee: One Honest and Effective Way to Participate," *ABA Banking Journal*, 72, no. 4 (April 1980), p. 79.

18. If the congressman sets up the PAC as a nonfederal account, this problem is magnified because they then can accept corporate and union treasury money and unlimited personal contributions, too. Drew, *Politics and Money*, p. 127.

6

INDEPENDENT EXPENDITURES

An independent expenditure is an expenditure for communications expressly advocating the election or defeat of a clearly identified Federal candidate which is NOT made with the cooperation or consent of or in consultation with or at the request or suggestion of, any candidate or any of his/her agents or authorized committees. 11 C.F.R.§100.16.

Independent expenditures, therefore, are different from contributions in that they are not given directly to a candidate or to a campaign but rather are used to fund activities of either a positive or negative nature that are intended to influence the outcome of a campaign while remaining distinct and apart from it.

The difference between an independent expenditure and a contribution was dramatized by the Supreme Court's decision in *Buckley v. Valeo*, 424 U.S. 1 (1976). In its per curiam opinion, the Court held that limits could be placed by the federal government on contributions but not independent expenditures because the quantity of the independent expenditure and not simply the act of making the expenditure represented the opinion of the expender of the funds. Any limitations placed on the amount expended, therefore, would "impose direct and substantial restraints on the quantity of political speech" and infringe unconstitutionally on their First Amendment guarantees of freedom of speech, freedom of association, and the right to petition the government. Independent expenditures as direct expressions of political speech could be hampered or curtailed by financial limitations. To avoid stifling political speech, therefore, independent expenditures had to remain unfettered. Contribution ceilings, however, were upheld because the act of contributing rather than the amount of the contribution was viewed as the donor's statement of support for a candidate. Political communication and the First Amendment guarantees, thus, were unimpaired by restrictions pertaining to the amount of the contribution.[1]

While *Buckley* paved the way for the unlimited use of independent expenditures by political committees including separate, segregated funds such as corporate PACs, several other factors created a climate that made this financial vehicle attractive for political expression. Most important were the retention of FECA's contribution limits and the certainty of their continuation because of *Buckley*. These limits in conjunction with the nonproliferation amendments of FECA (1976), which closed the loophole for bypassing them by using multiple PACs with the same affiliation but having separate contribution ceilings on a per PAC basis, added to the attraction of the newly approved vehicle for providing a candidate with unlimited financial support.[2] In fact, some observers believe that there may be an inverse relationship between the level established for contribution ceilings and the extent to which independent expenditures are likely to be used to circumvent them. Reformers warn that lowering contribution limits could have the unintentional and undesirable side effect of increasing the amount of monies independently expended.[3]

Another factor which increased the attraction of independent expenditures was the public financing rule for presidential candidates which disqualified persons from receiving private contributions if they qualified for and accepted public funding. By virtue of being distinct from contributions, independent expenditures could still be used on behalf of a presidential candidate who was receiving federal financial support.[4] The increased amount of monies independently expended during presidential election cycles (see table 20) and the substantial percentage of this money spent on the presidential races themselves (73% in 1975–76; 86% in 1979–80; and 80% in 1983–84) attest to the advantage of independent expenditures for this purpose.[5]

Table 20
Independent Expenditures by Corporate PACs: An Absolute and Relative
Analysis by Election Cycle from 1978 to 1984

Election Cycle	Total Independent Expenditures	Independent Expenditures of Corporate PACs		
		$ Amount	% of Total	No. of Corporations
1977-78*	$ 95,106	$ 1,000	.01	1
1979-80	16,084,237	19,449	1.21	10
1981-82	5,849,120	12,284	.002	5
1983-84	21,025,134	1,864	.00	4

Source: U.S. Federal Election Commission, *FEC Index of Independent Expenditures*, 1977–1978, 1979–1980, and 1981–1982, for the respective election cycles. 1983–1984 figures are based on an FEC computer printout of independent expenditures dated March 5, 1985.
* These figures are accurate as of October 10, 1978.

Finally, independent expenditures were enticing because of the continued prohibition against the corporate use of treasury money to make contributions or expenditures, including independent ones, in federal election campaigns (11 C.F.R. §114.2 (b)). Corporations, however, while forbidden to make independent expenditures directly, had the ability to circumvent this restriction by making them indirectly through their affiliated PAC because they had the right to control their corporate PAC in much the same manner as any other part of the corporate enterprise (11 C.F.R. §114.5 (d)).[6]

The political climate created by the election finance reforms and the *Buckley* decision combined to make "the threat of independent expenditures . . . the bogeyman of American politics."[7] Table 20 clearly indicates that these fears are unfounded when directed at corporate PACs. Independent expenditures have gained little acceptance as a financial campaign vehicle for the vast majority of corporate PACs. Their popularity is found primarily among a few unaffiliated, ideological, or issue-oriented PACs which are willing to suffer public derision which corporate PACs cannot afford.[8]

Responses received from 128 of the PACs affiliated with *Fortune* corporations demonstrated their continued aversion to using independent expenditures. Only 16 of the respondents said that their corporate PAC would make any type of independent expenditure. Of these, only 7 were willing to entertain controversy by using independent expenditures in opposition to as well as in support of a candidate.[9]

Corporate PACs which refuse to become involved with independent expenditures often emphasize this by including in their bylaws a statement permitting the PAC to use its money only for contributions or explicitly prohibiting it from making independent expenditures. There are a variety of disadvantages ranging from altruistic to practical that make independent expenditures unattractive to corporate PACs despite the initial enticements for using them.

One which receives prominent attention is the increased administrative costs that will be incurred by the parent corporation. Political committees which use independent expenditures are required to make Schedule E reports to the FEC. These reports include an unitemized total of all independent expenditures of less than $200; itemized ones for each independent expenditure of $200 or more; certification of independence; the date, amount, and purpose of the independent expenditure; and the name and address of any office sought by the candidate targeted by the independent expenditure.[10] These record keeping and reporting requirements could require the assistance of additional staff and thus add to the company's expenses for the PAC. There also could be additional expenses incurred for attorneys in the event that there arose legal or definitional uncertainties concerning the categorization of an activity as an independent expenditure instead of as a contribution or vice versa.

The costs associated with independent expenditures also are increased because they are cumbersome and complicated in comparison to contributions. Whereas the latter only require that a check be drawn and delivered to the candidate or to the candidate's campaign committee, the former require special expertise for the development, funding, and production of an entire publicity campaign.[11] The additional cost of creating the advertisements to be funded by the independent expenditures also detracts from the monies available to the corporate PAC for other activities such as political education programs and may make it financially difficult to contribute to all candidates that the PAC would like to support directly.

Contributions also are preferred to independent expenditures by the candidates because they want to control all spending designed to help them.[12] Independent expenditures act as a "wild card" beyond the candidate's control and interfere with the confrontation between candidates.[13] In particular, candidates worry that even supportive independent expenditures will have unintended or injurious results for them because of their lack of coordination with their planned campaign.[14]

The "no contact" requirement also may be disadvantageous for the corporate PAC as well as the candidate. If lobbying activities are being carried out or are anticipated during the election cycle, the lack of coordination with a candidate may be hard to prove and also undesirable. However, Epstein claims the following:

While a PAC might be called upon at any time to prove the independence of an expenditure, if it acts with due caution, free from contaminating control or cooperation by the candidate or his (or her) representatives, it will likely be able to establish its independence, thereby escaping restrictions on its electoral outlays.[15]

Skeptics on this issue abound, however, because of the appearance of coordination that exists when there is extensive contact between professional staff of political committees and the campaigns of candidates they support,[16] because candidates and political committees frequently use common consultants and because the media can be used to relay relevant information between a candidate's campaign and a political committee.[17] Although these criticisms are primarily concerned with the activities of unaffiliated political committees which are ideological in nature and use independent expenditures extensively, they also can be used against corporate PACs using independent expenditures.

Independent expenditures used in opposition to a candidate create other, greater dangers for a corporate PAC because they "are much more visible than contributions, and if the wrong candidate wins, the group could find itself with an implacable enemy in office."[18] Corporate PACs, therefore, should not use independent expenditures in support of or in opposition to a candidate because they cannot afford to jeopardize their company's relationship with an elected official in this way.

Despite the legality of independent expenditures by corporate PACs, the wisdom of their use is doubtful because they are a mixed blessing. Although independent expenditures can be used in a positive manner by a corporate PAC which prefers political activism and wishes to advertise its position on an issue or a candidate, it is a dangerous and potentially adversarial route to follow, particularly if it is being used to circumvent contribution limits rather than to enhance public debate and enrich the vitality of the public policy process.[19] The advantages of having no ceiling restricting the corporate PACs use of independent expenditures and the PAC's ability to act as a surrogate for its parent corporation in an otherwise prohibited activity are offset by an extensive array of disadvantages. PACs with economic interests rather than ideological ones must be concerned with making friends and avoiding the creation of enemies. Independent expenditures do not assist the corporate PAC in achieving either goal.

Reflections upon the historical data as well as the responses of the *Fortune* firms diminish the concern about the extensive use of independent expenditures by corporate PACs. As representatives of their parent corporation in the public mind, corporate PACs cannot afford to engage in an activity with questionable benefits while making their company vulnerable to adverse public reaction. They appear to know this already and to act accordingly.

NOTES

1. *Buckley v. Valeo*, 424 U.S. 20, 21 and 39 (1976). Additional discussion of this case is found in chapter 2.

2. Larry Light et al., "Surge in Independent Campaign Spending," *Congressional Quarterly Weekly Report*, 38, no. 24 (June 14, 1980), pp. 1638–1639.

3. U.S. Congress, *An Analysis of the Impact of the Federal Election Act, 1972–78*, p. 5.

4. Drew, *Politics and Money*, p. 99; and Susan G. Sendrow, "The Federal Election Campaign Act and Presidential Election Campaign Fund Act: Problems in Defining and Regulating Independent Expenditures," *Arizona State Law Journal*, 1981, no. 4 (1981), p. 982.

5. Light et al., "Surge in Independent Campaign Spending," p. 1635; and FEC Computer printout dated December 10, 1984, of independent expenditures for 1983–1984.

6. Vandegrift, "The Corporate Political Action Committee," pp. 433, 459. Not all scholars agree that 11 C.F.R. §114.2 (b) prohibits the use of corporate treasury monies being expended independently. In an article

concerning FECA (1976), Mazo notes that the Federal Corrupt Practices Act (FCPA) distinguished between expenditures and independent expenditures and forbade only the former explicitly. Nonetheless, he concludes that the FEC's regulations in 11 C.F.R. make it legally risky for a corporation to become directly involved with independent expenditures. Mazo, "Impact on Corporations of the 1976 Amendments to the Federal Election Campaign Act," pp. 448–449.

7. Richard P. Conlon, "Commentaries," in *Parties, Interest Groups and Campaign Finance Laws*, ed. Malbin, p. 190.

8. Alexander, *Financing the 1980 Election*, pp. 387–388.

9. Until the 1982 election cycle, no corporate PAC funds were independently expended in opposition to a candidate. In that election cycle, however, one corporate PAC (PAPA GINOS 128 PAC) spent $1,368 in opposition to a Democratic House candidate. This amount represented .0003 of the total $4,597,080 independently expended in opposition to candidates during that two-year period.

10. U.S. Federal Election Commission, *Index of Independent Expenditures*, August 1982.

11. Light et al., "Surge in Independent Campaign Spending," pp. 1636–1639.

12. *Ibid.*, p. 1636.

13. Rothenberg, *Campaign Regulation and Public Policy*, p. 46.

14. Sendrow, "The Federal Election Campaign Act and Presidential Election Campaign Fund Act," p. 988.

15. Edwin M. Epstein, "Corporations and Labor Unions in Electoral Politics," *The Annals*, 425 (May 1976), p. 51.

16. Andrew P. Buchsbaum, "Campaign Finance Re-Reform: The Regulation of Independent Committees," *California Law Review*, 71, no. 2 (March 1983), p. 701; and Kendall, "Corporate PACs: Step-by-Step Formation and Troublefree Operation," p. 18.

17. Drew, *Politics and Money*, pp. 136, 139.

18. Conlon, "Commentaries," in *Parties, Interest Groups and Campaign Finance Laws*, ed. Malbin, p. 190.

19. S. Prakash Sethi, "Corporate Political Activism," *California Management Review*, 24, no. 3 (Spring 1982), p. 40.

7

CONCLUSIONS

The litany of arguments for and against corporate PACs assumes that corporations are taking full advantage of the PAC phenomenon. This study has revealed that this is an erroneous assumption. A majority of corporations, including most of the nation's largest companies, have not established PACs and have no plans to do so. Many corporations have registered PACs which are politically dormant or inactive. Others have PACs that do not take full advantage of their solicitation privileges, thus preventing themselves from fully developing their potential financial strength. Large, rapidly growing PACs are clearly the exception and not the rule. Nonetheless, they are presented to the public as being representative of all corporate PACs and a threat to our political system.

In addition to denying themselves the attainment of their maximum growth potential, the vast majority of active corporate PACs have participated in the financing of federal election campaigns in a restrained and nonabusive fashion. They have abided by the spirit as well as the letter of the law and rarely have used professionally designed or sophisticated strategies to increase their own political effectiveness. Either consciously or inadvertently, corporate PACs have been equally conservative in the tactics they have employed and in the philosophy they have sought among their selected candidates. Individuals have received support from corporate PACs on the basis of incumbency or party when a broader and more varied contribution pattern might have improved their public image along with their political influence.

Corporate PACs cannot make a contribution to the democratic process unless they expand their activities. This can and must be done without offending public sensitivities. For instance, PAC membership should be made available to all employees and share-holders within legal boundaries although their response rates may vary. PACs then will become a vehicle for expanded political participation while simultaneously increasing their own financial strength. PAC funds should be used to inform and involve corporate employees through political education programs and internal communications. A well-informed internal electorate is more likely to contribute voluntarily to the PAC. More democratic methods for selecting the candidates to receive PAC funds also would stimulate greater participation. Outside agencies should be employed to collect the voluntary contributions made to the PAC for the protection of employees' privacy and for the enhancement of the PAC's reputation.

Corporations should address the issue of corporate responsibility directly by informing the public of their activities. They should do more than provide counterarguments to offset one-sided criticisms. The public should be told that loopholes for bypassing contribution ceilings are not being used, let alone abused. Greater emphasis should be given to the fact that the contribution ceilings themselves rarely are approached in corporate PAC giving. By emphasizing those aspects of corporate PAC activity that enhance the democratic process and do not threaten the equilibrium of American politics, corporations can use their PACs to legitimize their own political role.

As long as the legitimacy of corporate involvement in politics is disputed, the proper role of corporate PACs in financing federal election campaigns will be debated and unresolved. Denied legitimate political paths for effectuating their economic goals and stating their socio-political concerns, some corporations have resorted to activities and practices which further damaged their integrity in the eyes of the public and provided justification for their continued exclusion from direct financial involvement in federal elections.

Corporate PACs were intended to be a reform measure that would give corporations a means for expressing their views and advocating their interests indirectly in federal election campaigns. The political process was to be safeguarded from this new corporate participation through contribution limits, disclosure requirements, and solicitation protections for employees. The underlying public suspicion of corporate wealth and power more than the activities of corporate PACs, however, have caused this reform to exacerbate rather than relieve the problem faced by corporations in becoming accepted participants in federal election campaigns.

PACs are a privilege, not a right, of corporations. As such, they will be allowed to exist unencumbered only if the electorate believes that they are concerned about the public interest as well as their own narrower interests. As stated by Brenner,

Business must realize that in the long run, society, through its political process, legitimizes only those institutions that function for the benefit of society as a whole. Any individual company or industry that seeks to achieve solely its own self-interest without determining that its goals are compatible with the general public interest is likely to be an unwelcome participant in the nation's political processes, restricted from involvement in them.[1]

Most corporate leaders are cognizant that just as the decline of free economic markets and the competitive balance among economic interests led to antitrust restrictions on corporations, an erosion of the free market for political ideas and the political balance necessary to defend pluralism and democracy could bring legislation to curtail or to repeal corporate PACs. The political process and the corporate community both would suffer if extremism from either source caused this to occur.

NOTE

1. Brenner, "Business and Politics—An Update," p. 163.

Appendix 1

1983 *FORTUNE* 500 INDUSTRIAL COMPANIES

Note numbers are in parentheses.

Number of
Affiliated PACs
June 30, 1983

```
ACF Industries---------------------------------- 1
AM International-------------------------------- 0
AMAX------------------------------------------- 1
AMF-------------------------------------------- 0
AMP-------------------------------------------- 0
Abbott Laboratories---------------------------- 1
Agway (1)-------------------------------------- 1
Air Products & Chemicals----------------------- 1
Airco------------------------------------------ 1
Alleghany International------------------------- 2
Allied----------------------------------------- 1
Allis-Chalmers (9)----------------------------- 2
Alumax----------------------------------------- 0
Aluminum Company of America-------------------- 1
Amdahl (3)------------------------------------- 0
Amerada Hess----------------------------------- 0
American Bakeries------------------------------ 0
American Brands-------------------------------- 0
American Can----------------------------------- 1
American Cyanamid------------------------------ 1
American Greetings----------------------------- 0
American Hoechst------------------------------- 0
American Hoist & Derrick----------------------- 0
American Home Products------------------------- 1
American Motors-------------------------------- 1
American Petrofina----------------------------- 1
American Standard------------------------------ 1
Ametek (3)------------------------------------- 0
Amstar----------------------------------------- 0
Amsted Industries------------------------------ 1
Anchor Hocking--------------------------------- 1
Anderson Clayton------------------------------- 0
Anheuser-Busch--------------------------------- 1
Apple Computer (3)----------------------------- 0
Archer Daniels Midland------------------------- 1
Armco------------------------------------------ 1
Armstrong Rubber------------------------------- 0
Armstrong World Industries--------------------- 0
Arvin Industries------------------------------- 1
Asarco----------------------------------------- 1
Ashland Oil------------------------------------ 1
Atlantic Richfield----------------------------- 1
Avery International----------------------------- 0
Avon Products---------------------------------- 2
BASF Wyandotte--------------------------------- 0
```

```
                                                 Number of
                                            Affiliated PACs
                                              June 30, 1983
Baker International----------------------------- 0
Ball-------------------------------------------- 1
Bangor Punta------------------------------------ 2
Barnes Group------------------------------------ 0
Bausch & Lomb----------------------------------- 0
Baxter Travenol Laboratories-------------------- 1
Beatrice Foods (5)------------------------------ 0
Becton Dickinson-------------------------------- 1
Bell & Howell----------------------------------- 0
Bemis------------------------------------------- 0
Bendix (2)-------------------------------------- 1
Bethlehem Steel--------------------------------- 1
Big Three Industries---------------------------- 0
Black & Decker Manufacturing-------------------- 0
Blue Bell--------------------------------------- 1
Boeing------------------------------------------ 1
Boise Cascade----------------------------------- 1
Borden------------------------------------------ 1
Borg-Warner------------------------------------- 1
Briggs & Stratton------------------------------- 0
Bristol Myers----------------------------------- 1
Brockway---------------------------------------- 1
Brown-Forman Distillers------------------------- 1
Brunswick--------------------------------------- 1
Bucyrus-Erie------------------------------------ 0
Burlington Industries--------------------------- 2
Burroughs--------------------------------------- 0
Butler Manufacturing (3)------------------------ 0
CBI Industries---------------------------------- 1
CF Industries (1)------------------------------- 1
CPC International-------------------------------- 0
Cabot------------------------------------------- 1
Cameron Iron Works------------------------------ 1
Campbell Soup----------------------------------- 0
Capital Cities Communications------------------- 0
Carnation--------------------------------------- 1
Carpenter Technology---------------------------- 1
Caterpillar Tractor----------------------------- 1
Ceco-------------------------------------------- 0
Celanese---------------------------------------- 1
Central Soya------------------------------------ 1
Certain Teed------------------------------------ 0
Cessna Aircraft--------------------------------- 0
Champion International--------------------------- 1
Champion Spark Plugs---------------------------- 0
Charter----------------------------------------- 1
Chesebrough-Pond's------------------------------ 0
Chromalloy American----------------------------- 1
Chrysler---------------------------------------- 1
```

Number of
Affiliated PACs
June 30, 1983

```
Cincinnati Milacron------------------------------ 1
Clark Equipment---------------------------------- 1
Clorox------------------------------------------- 1
Cluett Peabody----------------------------------- 0
Coastal------------------------------------------ 1
Coca-Cola---------------------------------------- 1
Coleco Industries (3)---------------------------- 0
Colgate-Palmolive-------------------------------- 0
Collins & Aikman--------------------------------- 1
Colt Industries---------------------------------- 1
Combustion Engineering--------------------------- 1
Con Agra----------------------------------------- 1
Cone Mills--------------------------------------- 0
Consolidated Foods------------------------------- 0
Consolidated Papers------------------------------ 0
Continental Group (7)---------------------------- 7
Control Data------------------------------------- 0
Cooper Industries-------------------------------- 1
Cooper Tire & Rubber (3)------------------------- 0
Coors (Adolph)----------------------------------- 1
Corning Glass Works------------------------------ 1
Crane-------------------------------------------- 0
Crown Central Petroleum-------------------------- 0
Crown Cork & Seal-------------------------------- 0
Crown Zellerbach--------------------------------- 1
Cummins Engine----------------------------------- 0
Cyclops------------------------------------------ 1
Dan River---------------------------------------- 1
Dana--------------------------------------------- 1
Dart & Kraft------------------------------------- 1
Data General------------------------------------- 0
Datapoint (3)------------------------------------ 1
Dayco-------------------------------------------- 1
Dean Foods--------------------------------------- 1
Deere-------------------------------------------- 2
Deluxe Check Printers---------------------------- 0
Dennison Manufacturing--------------------------- 1
Dexter------------------------------------------- 1
Diamond Shamrock--------------------------------- 1
Diebold (3)-------------------------------------- 0
Digital Equipment-------------------------------- 0
Donnelly (R. R.) & Sons-------------------------- 1
Dorsey------------------------------------------- 0
Dover-------------------------------------------- 0
Dow Chemical------------------------------------- 9
Dow Corning-------------------------------------- 2
Dow Jones---------------------------------------- 0
Dr. Pepper (3)----------------------------------- 1
Dresser Industries------------------------------- 1
DuPont (E. I.) de Nemours------------------------ 0
```

Number of
Affiliated PACs
June 30, 1983

```
EG & G------------------------------------------ 1
E-Systems--------------------------------------- 7
Eagle-Pitcher Industries------------------------ 0
Easco (3)--------------------------------------- 0
Eastman Kodak----------------------------------- 1
Eaton------------------------------------------- 1
Echlin (3)-------------------------------------- 1
Economics Laboratory---------------------------- 1
Emerson Electric-------------------------------- 1
Emhart------------------------------------------ 0
Englehard--------------------------------------- 1
Esmark (5)-------------------------------------- 1
Ethyl------------------------------------------- 1
Ex-Cell-O--------------------------------------- 1
Exxon------------------------------------------- 1
FMC--------------------------------------------- 1
Fairchild--------------------------------------- 1
Farmers' Union Central-------------------------- 1
Federal Co.------------------------------------- 0
Federal-Mogul----------------------------------- 1
Federal Paper Board----------------------------- 0
Ferro------------------------------------------- 0
Fieldcrest Mills-------------------------------- 1
Figgie International---------------------------- 1
Firestone Tire & Rubber------------------------- 0
Fleetwood Enterprises (3)----------------------- 1
Flowers Industries (3)-------------------------- 1
Ford Motor-------------------------------------- 1
Fort Howard Paper------------------------------- 1
Foster Wheeler---------------------------------- 0
Foxboro----------------------------------------- 0
Frederick & Herrud------------------------------ 0
Freeport-McMoRan-------------------------------- 1
Fruehauf---------------------------------------- 1
Fuqua Industries-------------------------------- 0
GAF--------------------------------------------- 0
GATX-------------------------------------------- 1
Gannett----------------------------------------- 0
Gates Learjet----------------------------------- 2
General Cinema---------------------------------- 0
General Dynamics-------------------------------- 1
General Electric-------------------------------- 2
General Foods----------------------------------- 0
General Instrument------------------------------ 0
General Mills----------------------------------- 2
General Motors---------------------------------- 1
General Signal---------------------------------- 0
General Tire & Rubber--------------------------- 3
Genesco----------------------------------------- 0
Georgia Kraft----------------------------------- 1
```

Georgia-Pacific Corp.----------------------------- 1
Geosource-- 1
Gerber Products---------------------------------- 0
Getty Oil-- 2
Gifford-Hill------------------------------------- 1
Gillette--- 0
Gold Kist (1)------------------------------------ 1
Goodrich (B. F.)--------------------------------- 1
Goodyear Tire & Rubber--------------------------- 1
Gould-- 1
Grace (W. R.)------------------------------------ 1
Great Northern Nekoosa--------------------------- 1
Greyhound-- 1
Grumman-- 1
Gulf Oil--- 1
Gulf & Western Industries------------------------ 0
Hammermill Paper--------------------------------- 1
Handy & Harman----------------------------------- 0
Hanson Industries-------------------------------- 0
Harcourt Brace Jovanovich------------------------ 1
Harnischfeger------------------------------------ 0
Harris--- 1
Harsco--- 1
Hart Schaffner & Marx---------------------------- 0
Heileman (G.) Brewing---------------------------- 1
Heinz (H. J.)------------------------------------ 0
Hercules--- 1
Hershey Foods------------------------------------ 0
Heublein--- 1
Hewlett-Packard---------------------------------- 0
Holly (3)-- 0
Honeywell-- 5
Hoover--- 0
Hoover Universal--------------------------------- 0
Hormel (Geo. A.)--------------------------------- 0
Household Manufacturing-------------------------- 0
Hughes Tool-------------------------------------- 1
Hyster--- 0
IC Industries (11)------------------------------- 5
INTERCO-- 0
Idle Wild Foods---------------------------------- 0
Illinois Tool Works------------------------------ 1
Ingersoll-Rand----------------------------------- 2
Inland Steel------------------------------------- 1
Insilco-- 0
Intel-- 1
Interlake-- 1
International Business Machines------------------- 0
International Flavors & Fragrances (3)------ 0
International Harvester-------------------- 1

```
                                              Number of
                                          Affiliated PACs
                                           June 30, 1983
International Minerals & Chemicals---------- 1
International Multifoods-------------------- 1
International Paper------------------------- 1
International Telephone & Telegraph--------- 1
Interstate Bakeries------------------------ 0
James River Corp. of Virginia-------------- 0
Johnson Controls--------------------------- 0
Johnson & Johnson-------------------------- 1
Joy Manufacturing-------------------------- 0
Kaiser Aluminum & Chemical----------------- 1
Kaiser Steel------------------------------- 1
Kane-Miller-------------------------------- 0
Kellogg------------------------------------ 1
Kellwood----------------------------------- 1
Kerr Glass Manufacturing------------------- 0
Kerr-McGee--------------------------------- 1
Kidde-------------------------------------- 0
Kimberley-Clark---------------------------- 1
Knight-Ridder Newspapers------------------- 0
Knudson------------------------------------ 1
Koppers------------------------------------ 1
LTV (8) ----------------------------------- 4
Land O'Lakes------------------------------- 1
Lear Siegler------------------------------- 1
Lever Brothers----------------------------- 0
Levi Strauss------------------------------- 0
Libbey-Owens-Ford-------------------------- 1
Lilly (Eli)-------------------------------- 1
Lipton (Thomas J.)------------------------- 0
Liquid Air (3)----------------------------- 0
Litton Industries-------------------------- 1
Lockheed----------------------------------- 1
Lone Star Industries----------------------- 1
Louisiana Land & Exploration--------------- 0
Louisiana-Pacific-------------------------- 1
Lowenstein (M.)---------------------------- 0
Lubrizol----------------------------------- 0
M/A-Com------------------------------------ 0
MAPCO-------------------------------------- 1
MEI (3) ----------------------------------- 0
Magic Chef--------------------------------- 1
Manville----------------------------------- 1
Marion------------------------------------- 1
Marmon Group------------------------------- 0
Martin Marietta---------------------------- 1
Maryland Corp------------------------------ 0
Masco-------------------------------------- 0
Masonite----------------------------------- 0
Mattel------------------------------------- 0
Maytag (3) -------------------------------- 1
```

Number of
Affiliated PACs
June 30, 1983

McCormick--- 1
McDermott--- 2
McDonnell Douglas--------------------------------- 1
McGraw-Edison------------------------------------- 1
McGraw-Hill--------------------------------------- 0
Mead (10)--- 2
Media General (3)--------------------------------- 0
Merck--- 1
Meredith (3)-------------------------------------- 1
Mid-American Dairymen (1)------------------------- 1
Midland-Ross-------------------------------------- 0
Miles Laboratories-------------------------------- 1
Minnesota Mining & Manufacturing------------------ 1
Mitchell Energy & Development--------------------- 1
Mobay Chemical------------------------------------ 0
Mobil (12)-- 3
Mohasco--- 0
Monfort of Colorado------------------------------- 0
Monsanto-- 1
Moore McCormack Resources------------------------- 1
Morton Norwick Products--------------------------- 1
Motorola-- 1
Murphy Oil-- 1
NCR--- 1
NL Industries------------------------------------- 1
NVF--- 0
Nabisco Brands------------------------------------ 1
Nalco Chemical------------------------------------ 1
Nashua-- 0
National Can-------------------------------------- 1
National Co-Op Refinery Association--------------- 0
National Distillers & Chemical-------------------- 0
National Gypsum----------------------------------- 1
National Semiconductor---------------------------- 1
National Service Industries----------------------- 0
National Starch & Chemical------------------------ 0
National Steel------------------------------------ 2
Natomas--- 0
New York Times------------------------------------ 0
Newmont Mining------------------------------------ 0
North American Coal (3)--------------------------- 1
North American Philips---------------------------- 0
Northrop-- 1
Northwest Industries------------------------------ 0
Norton-- 0
Norton Simon (5)---------------------------------- 1
Nucor--- 0
Oak Industries------------------------------------ 1
Occidental Petroleum------------------------------ 1
Ogden--- 1

```
                                         Number of
                                     Affiliated PACs
                                     June 30, 1983
Olin-------------------------------------------- 1
Outboard Marine-------------------------------- 0
Owens-Corning Fiberglas------------------------ 0
Owens-Illinois--------------------------------- 1
Oxford Industries (3)-------------------------- 0
PACCAR----------------------------------------- 1
PPG Industries-------------------------------- 1
Pabst Brewing--------------------------------- 0
Pacific Resources----------------------------- 1
Palm Beach------------------------------------ 0
Parker-Hannifin------------------------------- 1
Peabody International------------------------- 1
Penn Central---------------------------------- 1
Pennwalt-------------------------------------- 0
Pennzoil-------------------------------------- 1
PepsiCo--------------------------------------- 1
Perkin-Elmer---------------------------------- 0
Pfizer---------------------------------------- 1
Phelps Dodge---------------------------------- 1
Philip Morris--------------------------------- 2
Phillips Petroleum---------------------------- 1
Phillips-Van Heusen (3)----------------------- 0
Pillsbury------------------------------------- 3
Pitney Bowes---------------------------------- 0
Polaroid-------------------------------------- 0
Porter (H. K.)-------------------------------- 0
Potlach--------------------------------------- 1
Prime Computer (3)---------------------------- 0
Procter & Gamble------------------------------ 0
Quaker Oats----------------------------------- 1
Quaker State Oil Refining--------------------- 1
Ralston Purina-------------------------------- 1
Rath Packing---------------------------------- 0
Raychem--------------------------------------- 0
Raytheon-------------------------------------- 1
Reichhold Chemicals--------------------------- 0
Republic Steel-------------------------------- 1
Research-Cottrell----------------------------- 1
Revere Copper & Brass------------------------- 1
Revlon---------------------------------------- 0
Rexnord--------------------------------------- 1
Reynolds (R. J.) Industries------------------- 4
Reynolds Metals------------------------------- 1
Richardson-Vicks------------------------------ 1
Robertson (H. H.)----------------------------- 0
Robins (A. H.) (3)---------------------------- 0
Rockwell International------------------------ 1
Rohm & Haas----------------------------------- 1
Rohr Industries------------------------------- 1
Roper (3)------------------------------------- 0
```

Number of
Affiliated PACs
June 30, 1983

```
Royal Crown Companies (3) ------------------- 0
SCM ------------------------------------------ 1
St. Regis Paper ------------------------------ 0
Sanders Associates (3) ----------------------- 0
Savannah Foods & Industries ------------------ 1
Schering-Plough ------------------------------ 1
Scott & Foster ------------------------------- 0
Scott Paper ---------------------------------- 1
Scovill -------------------------------------- 0
Seagram (Joseph E.) & Sons ------------------- 1
Searle (G. D.) ------------------------------- 2
Shaklee -------------------------------------- 1
Shell Oil ------------------------------------ 1
Sheller-Globe -------------------------------- 0
Sherwin Williams ----------------------------- 0
Signal Companies (4) ------------------------- 2
Singer --------------------------------------- 0
Smith (A. O.) -------------------------------- 1
Smith International --------------------------- 0
Smith Kline Beckman -------------------------- 2
Snap-on Tools (3) ---------------------------- 0
Sonoco Products ------------------------------ 1
Southwest Forest Industries ------------------ 1
Sperry --------------------------------------- 1
Spring Industries ---------------------------- 1
Square D ------------------------------------- 1
Squibb --------------------------------------- 1
Staley (A. E.) Manufacturing ----------------- 1
Standard Oil of California ------------------- 1
Standard Oil (Indiana) ----------------------- 1
Standard Oil (Ohio) -------------------------- 2
Stanley Works -------------------------------- 1
Stauffer Chemical ---------------------------- 1
Sterling Drug -------------------------------- 1
Stevens (J. P.) ------------------------------ 1
Stokely-VanCamp ------------------------------ 1
Stone Container (3) -------------------------- 1
Storage Technology --------------------------- 0
Sun ------------------------------------------ 1
Sun Chemical --------------------------------- 1
Sun-Diamond Growers of California (1) -------- 2
Sundstrand ----------------------------------- 2
Superior Oil --------------------------------- 1
Swift Independent ---------------------------- 0
Sybrow --------------------------------------- 0
TRW ------------------------------------------ 1
Tecumseh Products ---------------------------- 0
Tektronix ------------------------------------ 0
Teledyne ------------------------------------- 0
Tenneco (13) --------------------------------- 2
```

```
                                              Number of
                                         Affiliated PACs
                                          June 30, 1983
Texaco------------------------------------------- 1
Texas Instruments------------------------------- 1
Textron----------------------------------------- 1
Time, Inc.-------------------------------------- 3
Times Mirror------------------------------------ 0
Timken------------------------------------------ 0
Todd Shipyards---------------------------------- .0
Tosco------------------------------------------- 1
Trane------------------------------------------- 1
Tribune----------------------------------------- 0
Trinity Industries------------------------------ 0
Tyco Laboratories (3)--------------------------- 0
Tyler------------------------------------------- 0
Tyson Foods------------------------------------- 0
Union Camp-------------------------------------- 1
Union Carbide----------------------------------- 1
Union Oil of California------------------------- 1
Union Pacific----------------------------------- 1
Uniroyal---------------------------------------- 1
United Brands----------------------------------- 1
United Merchants & Manufacturers---------------- 1
US Gypsum--------------------------------------- 0
US Industries----------------------------------- 0
US Steel---------------------------------------- 3
United Technologies----------------------------- 1
Universal Foods (3)----------------------------- 1
Upjohn------------------------------------------ 1
VF---------------------------------------------- 0
Varian Associates------------------------------- 0
Vulcan Materials-------------------------------- 1
Walter (Jim)------------------------------------ 1
Wang Laboratories------------------------------- 0
Warnaco----------------------------------------- 0
Warner Communications--------------------------- 1
Warner-Lambert---------------------------------- 0
Washington Post--------------------------------- 0
West Point-Pepperell---------------------------- 1
Western Electric (6)---------------------------- 1
Westinghouse Electric--------------------------- 1
Westmoreland Coal------------------------------- 0
Westvaco---------------------------------------- 1
Weyerhauser------------------------------------- 2
Wheelabrator-Frye (4)--------------------------- 1
Wheeling-Pittsburgh Steel----------------------- 1
Whirlpool--------------------------------------- 1
White Consolidated Industries------------------- 1
Willamette Industries--------------------------- 1
Williams Companies------------------------------ 2
Wilson Foods (8)-------------------------------- 1
Wisconsin Dairies Cooperative (3) and (1)-- 0
```

```
                                    Number of Affiliated PACs
                                         June 30, 1983
Witco Chemical ------------------------------------ 0
Worthington Industries (3) ------------------- 0
Wrigley (Wm. Jr.) --------------------------- 0
Wyman-Gordon ------------------------------- 1
Xerox -------------------------------------- 0
Zenith Radio ------------------------------- 0
```

NOTES

1. These companies are listed by the FEC as cooperatives, not cor-porations, and thus are not included in this study.

2. Allied Corp. purchased Bendix Corp. after 1982. In this study, therefore, they are considered separately. Heretofore they should be combined under Allied Corp.

3. These thirty-three corporations also appeared on the 1982 *Fortune* Second 500 Largest Industrials list. For purposes of this study, they are included among the 1983 *Fortune* 500 Industrial Companies.

4. Wheelabrator-Frye is included in this study as a separate corporation although it has become affiliated with Signal Companies which now appears to have three affiliated PACs rather than the two reflected in this study.

5. Beatrice Foods has acquired Esmark, but this occurred after 1982 and thus is not reflected in this study. Additionally, prior to this acquisition, Esmark had acquired Norton Simon.

6. Western Electric is a wholly owned subsidiary of AT&T and thus is analyzed within the utilities category of the *Fortune* 500 Largest Nonindustrials list.

7. Continental Group had only one affiliated PAC on June 30, 1983. In years past, however, it had as many as seven affiliated PACs.

8. Wilson Foods was a separate corporation in the 1978 and 1980 elections but was affiliated with LTV prior to the 1982 election. The study reflects this change.

9. Allis-Chalmers includes Siemens-Allis which also appears on the 1982 *Fortune* Second 500 Largest Industrials list.

10. Mead includes Brunswick Pulp and Paper which also appears on the 1982 *Fortune* Second 500 Largest Industrials list.

11. IC Industries includes Illinois Central Gulf Railroad which also appears on the 1983 *Fortune* 500 Largest Nonindustrials list under transportation.

12. Mobil includes Montgomery Ward which also appears on the 1983 *Fortune* 500 Largest Nonindustrials list under retail companies.

13. Tenneco includes Southwestern Life which also appears on the 1983 *Fortune* 500 Largest Nonindustrials list under life insurance companies.

Appendix 2

1982 *FORTUNE* SECOND 500 LARGEST INDUSTRIAL COMPANIES

Note numbers are in parentheses.

Number of
Affiliated PACs
June 30, 1983

```
AFG------------------------------------------------- 0
APL------------------------------------------------- 0
AVX------------------------------------------------- 0
Acme-Cleveland-------------------------------------- 0
Acton----------------------------------------------- 0
Adobe Oil & Gas------------------------------------- 0
Advanced Micro Devices------------------------------ 0
Aegis----------------------------------------------- 0
Affiliated Publications----------------------------- 0
Alabama By-Products--------------------------------- 1
Alaska Interstate----------------------------------- 0
Albany International-------------------------------- 0
Alberto-Culver-------------------------------------- 0
Allen Group----------------------------------------- 0
Allied Products------------------------------------- 0
Alton Packaging------------------------------------- 1
Amalgamated Sugar----------------------------------- 1
Amdahl (1)------------------------------------------ 0
Amerace--------------------------------------------- 0
American Biltrite----------------------------------- 0
American Business Products-------------------------- 0
American Crystal Sugar (2)-------------------------- 1
American Maize Products----------------------------- 0
American Shipbuilding------------------------------- 1
American Sterilizer--------------------------------- 0
American Welding & Manufacturing-------------------- 0
Ameron---------------------------------------------- 1
Ametek (1)------------------------------------------ 0
Analog Devices-------------------------------------- 0
Angelica-------------------------------------------- 0
Anta------------------------------------------------ 0
Anthony Industries---------------------------------- 1
Apple Computer (1)---------------------------------- 0
Applied Power--------------------------------------- 0
Associated Coca-Cola Bottling----------------------- 0
Athlone Industries---------------------------------- 0
Augat----------------------------------------------- 0
Automatic Switch------------------------------------ 0
Avondale Mills-------------------------------------- 1
BIC Pen--------------------------------------------- 0
Bacardi--------------------------------------------- 1
Bairnco--------------------------------------------- 0
Baldor Electric------------------------------------- 0
Bandag---------------------------------------------- 0
```

                                        Number of
                                    Affiliated PACs
                                    June 30, 1983

Banta (George)------------------------------- 0
Barber-Greene-------------------------------- 0
Bard (C. R.)--------------------------------- 0
Barry (R. G.)-------------------------------- 0
Barry Wright--------------------------------- 1
Bassett Furniture Industries----------------- 0
Bastian Industries--------------------------- 0
Beker Industries----------------------------- 1
Belo (A. H.)--------------------------------- 0
Betz Laboratories---------------------------- 0
Beverage Management-------------------------- 1
Bibb--- 0
Binks Manufacturing-------------------------- 0
Bird & Son----------------------------------- 0
Blair (John)--------------------------------- 0
Bliss & Laughlin Industries------------------ 0
Block Drug----------------------------------- 0
Blue Chip Stamps----------------------------- 0
Bob Evans Farms------------------------------ 0
Bobbie Brooks-------------------------------- 0
Bohemia-------------------------------------- 0
Brown (Tom)---------------------------------- 0
Brown & Sharpe Manufacturing----------------- 0
Brunswick Pulp and Paper (4)----------------- 1
Brush Wellman-------------------------------- 0
Bulova Watch--------------------------------- 0
Bundy-- 0
Burndy--------------------------------------- 0
Butler Manufacturing (1)--------------------- 0
CCI-- 0
CHB-- 0
CMI-- 0
CTS-- 0
Cadence Industries--------------------------- 0
Cagle's-------------------------------------- 0
California Portland Cement-------------------- 0
Camco-- 0
Carlisle------------------------------------- 0
Carter (William)----------------------------- 0
Carter-Wallace------------------------------- 0
Champion Home Builders----------------------- 0
Chase Bag------------------------------------ 0
Chatham Manufacturing------------------------ 0
Checker Motors------------------------------- 0
Chelsea Industries--------------------------- 0
Chesepeake Corp. of Virginia----------------- 0
Church & Dwight------------------------------ 0
Clark (J. L.) Manufacturing------------------ 0
Cleveland-Cliffs Iron------------------------ 1
Clow--- 0

Number of
Affiliated PACs
June 30, 1983

Coachman Industries------------------------ 0
Coca-Cola Bottling Co. Consolidated----------0
Coca-Cola Bottling of Miami----------------- 0
Coleco Industries (1)----------------------- 0
Coleman------------------------------------- 1
Combustion Equipment Associates------------- 0
Commerce Clearing House--------------------- 0
Commercial Shearing------------------------- 0
Commodore----------------------------------- 0
Compo Industries---------------------------- 0
Compugraphic-------------------------------- 0
Computervision------------------------------ 0
Condec-------------------------------------- 0
Conrac-------------------------------------- 0
Conrock------------------------------------- 0
Continental Copper & Steel Industries------- 0
Continental Steel--------------------------- 0
Conwood------------------------------------- 0
Cooper Laboratories------------------------- 0
Cooper Tire & Rubber (1)-------------------- 0
Core Industries----------------------------- 0
Courier------------------------------------- 0
Criton-------------------------------------- 1
Crompton------------------------------------ 0
Crompton & Knowles-------------------------- 0
Cronus Industries--------------------------- 0
Cross & Trecker----------------------------- 0
Crystal Oil--------------------------------- 0
Cubic--------------------------------------- 1
Curtiss-Wright------------------------------ 0
Dairylea Cooperative (2)-------------------- 1
Daniel Industries--------------------------- 0
Datapoint (1)------------------------------- 1
Dataproducts-------------------------------- 0
Dayton Malleable---------------------------- 0
De Tomaso Industries------------------------ 0
Dellwood Foods------------------------------ 0
Dentsply International---------------------- 0
DeSoto-------------------------------------- 0
Dibrell Brothers---------------------------- 0
Diebold (1)--------------------------------- 0
Dinner Bell Foods--------------------------- 0
Dixie Yarns--------------------------------- 0
Dominion Textiles (USA)--------------------- 0
Donaldson----------------------------------- 1
Dr. Pepper (1)------------------------------ 1
Duplex Products----------------------------- 0
Duriron------------------------------------- 1
Dynamics Corp. of America------------------- 0
Dyneer-------------------------------------- 0

```
                                              Number of
                                          Affiliated PACs
                                           June 30, 1983
Early California Industries----------------- 0
Easco (1)----------------------------------- 0
Eastmet------------------------------------- 0
Echlin (1)---------------------------------- 1
Elcor--------------------------------------- 0
Elixir Industries--------------------------- 0
Energy Reserves Group----------------------- 0
Essex Chemical------------------------------ 0
Esterline----------------------------------- 0
Everest & Jennings International------------ 0
Faberge------------------------------------- 0
Facet Enterprises--------------------------- 0
Farah Manufacturing------------------------- 0
Farmer Bros.-------------------------------- 0
Fedders------------------------------------- 0
Federal Signal------------------------------ 0
First Mississippi--------------------------- 1
Fischer & Porter---------------------------- 0
Fleetwood Enterprises (1)------------------- 1
Florida Rock Industries--------------------- 1
Florida Steel------------------------------- 0
Flowers Industries (1)---------------------- 1
Fluke (John) Mfg.--------------------------- 0
Forest Oil---------------------------------- 1
Four-Phase Systems-------------------------- 0
Franklin Electric--------------------------- 1
Friona Industries--------------------------- 0
Fuller (H. B.)------------------------------ 0
GCA----------------------------------------- 0
GF Business Equipment----------------------- 0
Galaxy Carpet Mills------------------------- 0
Galveston-Houston--------------------------- 1
Garan--------------------------------------- 0
General American Oil Co. of Texas----------- 0
General Automation-------------------------- 0
General Binding----------------------------- 0
General Felt Industries--------------------- 0
General Portland---------------------------- 0
General Refractories------------------------ 0
General Steel Industries-------------------- 0
Genessee Brewing---------------------------- 0
GenRad-------------------------------------- 0
Gidding & Lewis----------------------------- 0
Glatfelter (P. H.)-------------------------- 0
Gleason Works------------------------------- 0
Glenmore Distilleries----------------------- 1
Goody Products------------------------------ 0
Goulds Pumps-------------------------------- 1
Graco--------------------------------------- 0
Graniteville-------------------------------- 1
```

Number of
Affiliated PACs
June 30, 1983

Great American Industries------------------ 0
Great Lakes Chemical---------------------- 1
Greif Burns------------------------------- 0
Grolier----------------------------------- 0
Grow Group-------------------------------- 0
Guardian Industries----------------------- 0
Guilford Mills---------------------------- 0
Gulton Industries------------------------- 0
Halstead Industries----------------------- 0
Hanna Mining------------------------------ 1
Harland (John H.)------------------------- 1
Harper & Row------------------------------ 0
Harte-Hanks Communications---------------- 0
Harvey Hubbell---------------------------- 0
Hayes Albion------------------------------ 0
Hazeltine--------------------------------- 1
Helene Curtis Industries------------------ 0
Herman Miller----------------------------- 0
Hesston----------------------------------- 0
Hexcel------------------------------------ 0
Hillenbrand Industries-------------------- 0
Holly (1)--------------------------------- 0
Holly Sugar------------------------------- 0
Homestake Mining-------------------------- 1
Hon Industries---------------------------- 0
Houghton Mifflin-------------------------- 0
Howell------------------------------------ 1
Huffy------------------------------------- 1
Ideal Toy--------------------------------- 0
Illini Beef Packers----------------------- 0
Imperial Sugar---------------------------- 0
Inexco Oil-------------------------------- 0
Inspiration Consolidated Copper----------- 1
Instrument Systems------------------------ 0
Instrumentation Laboratories-------------- 0
Intercraft Industries--------------------- 0
Intermark--------------------------------- 0
Intermedics------------------------------- 0
International Banknote--------------------- 0
International Controls--------------------- 0
International Flavors & Fragrances (1)----- 0
International Rectifier-------------------- 0
Interpace--------------------------------- 0
Iroquois Brands--------------------------- 0
Itek-------------------------------------- 1
Jonathan Logan---------------------------- 0
Joslyn Mfg. & Supply---------------------- 0
Jostens----------------------------------- 1
Justin Industries------------------------- 1
KDI--------------------------------------- 0

Number of
Affiliated PACs
June 30, 1983

Kaiser Cement------------------------------------ 1
Katy Industries---------------------------------- 0
Kearney-National--------------------------------- 0
Keller Industries-------------------------------- 0
Kennametal--------------------------------------- 0
Keuffel & Esser---------------------------------- 0
Keystone Consolidated Industries------------ 0
Keystone Foods Corp.----------------------- 0
Keystone International---------------------- 0
Kimball International----------------------- 0
King-Seeley Thermos------------------------- 0
Kollmorgen--------------------------------------- 0
Krueger (W. A.)---------------------------------- 0
Kuhlman-- 0
Kysor Industrial--------------------------------- 0
Laclede Steel------------------------------------ 0
Lamson & Sessions-------------------------------- 0
Lancaster Colony--------------------------------- 0
Lance-- 0
Lane--- 0
La-Z-Boy Chair----------------------------------- 0
Lea Ronal-- 0
Lee Enterprises---------------------------------- 0
Leggett & Platt---------------------------------- 0
Lenox-- 1
Leslie Fay--------------------------------------- 0
Liquid Air (1)----------------------------------- 0
Loctite-- 1
Longview Fibre----------------------------------- 0
Loral-- 0
Lufkin Industries-------------------------------- 0
Lukens Steel------------------------------------- 1
MCO Holdings------------------------------------- 0
MEI (1)-- 0
MacAndrews & Forbes Group------------------- 0
Macmillan Ring-Free Oil--------------------- 0
Management Assistance----------------------- 0
Manhattan Industries------------------------ 0
Manitowoc-- 0
Marcade Group------------------------------------ 0
Mark Controls------------------------------------ 0
Mary Kay Cosmetics------------------------------- 0
Masland (C. H.) & Sons----------------------- 0
Maytag (1)--------------------------------------- 1
McDonough-- 0
Mc Neil-- 0
McQuay-Perfex------------------------------------ 0
Medalist Industries------------------------- 0
Medford-- 1
Media General (1)-------------------------------- 0

```
                                           Number of
                                      Affiliated PACs
                                      June 30, 1983
Medtronic------------------------------------------- 0
Meredith-------------------------------------------- 1
Michigan General------------------------------------ 0
Mesa Petroleum-------------------------------------- 0
Midland Glass--------------------------------------- 0
Millipore------------------------------------------- 0
Milton Bradley-------------------------------------- 0
Mine Safety Appliances------------------------------ 0
Mirro----------------------------------------------- 0
Mississippi Chemical-------------------------------- 1
Modine Manufacturing-------------------------------- 1
Mohawk Data Sciences-------------------------------- 0
Mohawk Rubber--------------------------------------- 0
Molex----------------------------------------------- 0
Monarch Machine Tool-------------------------------- 0
Monogram Industries--------------------------------- 0
Moog------------------------------------------------ 0
Mor-Flo Industries---------------------------------- 0
Mount Vernon Mills---------------------------------- 0
Munsingwear----------------------------------------- 0
Murray Ohio Mfg.------------------------------------ 1
NCH------------------------------------------------- 0
NIBCO----------------------------------------------- 0
National Grape Cooperative Assn. (2)---------------- 1
National Mine Service------------------------------- 0
National-Standard----------------------------------- 0
Newell Companies------------------------------------ 0
Newpark Resources----------------------------------- 0
Nordson--------------------------------------------- 0
Norlin Industries----------------------------------- 0
Nortek---------------------------------------------- 0
North American Coal (1)------------------------------ 1
Noxell---------------------------------------------- 0
Ocean Spray Cranberries----------------------------- 1
Oglebay Morton-------------------------------------- 0
Olympia Brewing------------------------------------- 0
Omark Industries------------------------------------ 0
Oneida---------------------------------------------- 1
Overhead Door--------------------------------------- 0
Oxford Industries (1)------------------------------- 0
Pacific Lumber-------------------------------------- 0
Pall------------------------------------------------ 0
Pantasote------------------------------------------- 0
Papercraft------------------------------------------ 0
Paradyne-------------------------------------------- 0
Park-Ohio Industries-------------------------------- 0
Pauley Petroleum------------------------------------ 0
Pengo Industries------------------------------------ 0
Pentair--------------------------------------------- 0
Petro-Lewis----------------------------------------- 1
```

Petrolite	0
Pettibone	0
Philips Industries	1
Phillips-VanHeusen (1)	0
Phoenix Steel	0
Pierce (S. S.)	0
Pirelli Cable	0
Pittsburgh-Des Moines	1
Pittway	0
Pogo Producing	1
Polychrome	0
Pope & Talbot	0
Portec	0
Pratt & Lambert	0
Prentice-Hall	0
Prime Computer (1)	0
Publicker Industries	0
Puritan Fashions	0
Quanex	0
Questor	1
ROLM	1
RSR	0
RTE	0
Ranco	0
Ransburg	0
Raybestos-Manhattan	0
Recognition Equipment	0
Redman Industries	0
Reeves Brothers	0
Refinemet International	0
Republic	0
Rexham	0
Reynolds & Reynolds	0
Richmond Tank Car	0
Robbins & Myers	0
Robertshaw Controls	0
Robins (A. H.) (1)	0
Robintech	0
Roblin Industries	1
Rochester & Pittsburgh Coal	1
Roper (1)	0
Rorer Group	1
Royal Crown Companies (1)	0
Rubbermaid	0
Russ Togs	0
Russell	1
SFN Companies	0
SPS Technologies	0
Sabine	0
Safeguard Business Systems	0

                                              Number of
                                          Affiliated PACs
                                           June 30, 1983

Salant-- 0
Salem Carpet Mills-------------------------------- 0
Sanders Associates (1)---------------------------- 0
Scherer (R. P.)----------------------------------- 0
Scholastic-- 0
Scientific-Atlanta-------------------------------- 0
Seaboard Allied Milling--------------------------- 0
Sealaska-- 0
Sealed Power-------------------------------------- 1
Shaw Industries----------------------------------- 0
Siemens-Allis (3)--------------------------------- 1
Sigma-Aldrich------------------------------------- 0
Simmonds Precision Products----------------------- 0
Skyline--- 0
Smithfield Foods---------------------------------- 0
Smucker (J. M.)----------------------------------- 0
Snap-on Tools (1)--------------------------------- 0
Soundesign-- 0
Southdown--- 0
Southland Royalty--------------------------------- 1
Sparton--- 2
Spectra-Physics----------------------------------- 0
Stanadyne--- 1
Standard Commercial Tobacco----------------------- 0
Standard-Coosa Thatcher--------------------------- 0
Standard Motor Products--------------------------- 0
Standard Products--------------------------------- 0
Standard Register--------------------------------- 0
Standex International----------------------------- 0
Stanley Home Products----------------------------- 0
Sta-Rite-- 0
Starrett (L. S.)---------------------------------- 0
Steiger Tractor----------------------------------- 0
Stepan Chemical----------------------------------- 0
Stewart & Stevenson Services---------------------- 0
Stewart-Warner------------------------------------ 1
Stone Container (1)------------------------------- 1
Stride Rite--------------------------------------- 0
Sullair--- 0
Sun Electric-------------------------------------- 0
Swank--- 0
TMC Industries------------------------------------ 0
TRE--- 0
Tacoma Boatbuilding------------------------------- 0
Talley Industries--------------------------------- 1
Tampax-- 0
Tandem Computers---------------------------------- 0
Tasty Baking-------------------------------------- 0
Telex--- 0
Teradyne-- 0

```
                                         Number of
                                      Affiliated PACs
                                       June 30, 1983
Texas Industries----------------------------------- 0
Texas International-------------------------------- 0
Texfi Industries----------------------------------- 0
Thermo Electron------------------------------------ 0
Thomas & Betts------------------------------------- 0
Thomas Industries---------------------------------- 0
Thomaston Mills------------------------------------ 0
Ti-Caro-------------------------------------------- 1
Tokheim-------------------------------------------- 0
Tomlinson Oil-------------------------------------- 0
Toro----------------------------------------------- 1
Towle Manufacturing-------------------------------- 0
Tracor--------------------------------------------- 0
Transamerica Delaval------------------------------- 0
Triangle Industries-------------------------------- 0
Triangle Pacific----------------------------------- 0
Trico Industries----------------------------------- 0
Tultex--------------------------------------------- 0
Twin Disc------------------------------------------ 0
Tyco Laboratories (1)------------------------------ 0
UMC Industries------------------------------------- 0
UNC Resources-------------------------------------- 1
UNR Industries------------------------------------- 0
Unifi---------------------------------------------- 0
Unicon--------------------------------------------- 0
United Industrial---------------------------------- 0
U.S. Sugar----------------------------------------- 0
U.S. Tobacco--------------------------------------- 1
Universal Foods (1)-------------------------------- 1
Valley Industries---------------------------------- 0
Valmac Industries---------------------------------- 0
Valmont Industries--------------------------------- 1
Valspar-------------------------------------------- 0
Van Dorn------------------------------------------- 1
Varco International-------------------------------- 0
Vermont American----------------------------------- 0
Vernitron------------------------------------------ 0
Vulcan--------------------------------------------- 0
Walco National------------------------------------- 0
Wallace Business Forms----------------------------- 0
Warner Electric Brake & Clutch-------------- 0
Watkins-Johnson------------------------------------ 1
Wausau Paper Mills--------------------------------- 0
Wean United---------------------------------------- 0
Webb----------------------------------------------- 0
West----------------------------------------------- 0
Western Pacific Industries----------------- 0
Williamhouse-Regency------------------------------- 0
Winnego Industries--------------------------------- 0
Wisconsin Dairies Cooperative (1)----------- 0
```

```
                                    Number of
                                 Affiliated PACs
                                 June 30, 1983


Wolverine World Wide------------------------------ 1
Woodward Governor--------------------------------- 0
Work Wear----------------------------------------- 0
Worthington Industries (1)------------------------ 0
Wynn's International------------------------------ 0
Zurn Industries----------------------------------- 0
```

NOTES

1. Thirty-three companies appear on the 1982 *Fortune* Second 500 Largest Industrials list as well as the 1983 *Fortune* 500 Largest Industrials list. Although reflected on the former as well as the latter, they are studied only as part of the latter.

2. These companies are listed by the FEC as cooperatives, not corporations, and thus are not included in this study.

3. Siemens-Allis is affiliated with Allis-Chalmers which appears on the 1983 *Fortune* 500 Largest Industrials list. Although reflected here, Siemens-Allis, therefore, is studied as part of Allis-Chalmers.

4. Brunswick Pulp and Paper is an affiliate of Mead which is listed among the 1983 *Fortune* 500 Largest Industrials. Although reflected here, Brunswick Pulp and Paper, therefore, is studied as part of Mead.

Appendix 3

1983 *FORTUNE* 100 LARGEST BANK
HOLDING COMPANIES

Note numbers are in parentheses.

Number of
Affiliated PACs
June 30, 1983

Allied Bancshares------------------------------- 1
American Security Corp-------------------------- 1
Ameritrust Corp-------------------------------- 0
AmSouth Bancorp-------------------------------- 0
Banc One Corp---------------------------------- 1
Ban Cal Tri-State Corp-------------------------- 0
BancOhio Corp (4)------------------------------ 1
Bank of New York Co.--------------------------- 0
Bank of New England Corp----------------------- 0
Bank of Tokyo Trust---------------------------- 0
Bank of Virginia Co.--------------------------- 1
Bank America Corp------------------------------ 1
Bankers Trust New York Corp-------------------- 1
Barnett Banks of Florida----------------------- 1
Bay Banks-------------------------------------- 0
CBT Corp--------------------------------------- 1
California First Bank-------------------------- 0
Centerre Bancorp------------------------------- 1
Chase Manhattan Corp--------------------------- 1
Chemical New York Corp------------------------- 1
Citicorp--------------------------------------- 1
Citizens & Southern Georgia Corp-------------- 1
Comerica--------------------------------------- 1
Commerce Bancshares---------------------------- 1
Continental Illinois Corp---------------------- 1
Crocker National Corp-------------------------- 1
Dominion Bankshares---------------------------- 0
Equimark Corp---------------------------------- 1
European American Bancorp---------------------- 0
Fidelcor--------------------------------------- 1
Fidelity Union Bancorp------------------------- 1
First Atlanta Corp----------------------------- 1
First Bank System------------------------------ 5
First Chicago Corp (3)------------------------- 1
First City Bancorp of Texas-------------------- 1
First Interstate Bancorp----------------------- 1
First Maryland Bancorp------------------------- 0
First National Boston Corp--------------------- 1
First National State Bancorp------------------- 1
First of America Bank Corp--------------------- 0
First Oklahoma Bancorp------------------------- 0
First Pennsylvania Corp------------------------ 1
First Security Corp---------------------------- 1
First Tennessee National Corp------------------ 1

                                      Number of
                                 Affiliated PACs
                                  June 30, 1983

First Union Corp---------------------------------- 1
First Wisconsin Corp------------------------------ 1
Fleet Financial Group----------------------------- 0
Florida National Banks of Florida----------- 0
Girard (1)-- 1
Harris Bankcorp----------------------------------- 1
Hartford National Corp---------------------- 1
Huntington Bancshares (4)------------------- 1
InterFirst Corp----------------------------------- 0
IntraWest Financial Corp-------------------- 0
Irving Bank Corp---------------------------------- 1
Lincoln First Banks------------------------------- 1
Manufacturers Hanover Corp------------------ 1
Manufacturers National Corp (2)------------- 2
Marine Midland Banks------------------------------ 1
Maryland National Corp---------------------- 1
Mellon National Corp (1)-------------------- 1
Mercantile Bancorp-------------------------------- 1
Mercantile Texas Corp----------------------- 3
Michigan National Corp---------------------- 1
Midlantic Banks----------------------------------- 1
Morgan (J. P.) & Co.------------------------- 1
NBD Bancorp--------------------------------------- 1
NCHB Corp--- 1
National Bank of North America-------------- 1
National City Corp-------------------------------- 1
Norstar Bancorp----------------------------------- 1
Northern Trust Corp------------------------------- 1
Northwest Bancorp--------------------------------- 1
Philadelphia National Corp------------------ 2
Pittsburgh National Corp-------------------- 1
Provident National Corp-------------------- 1
Rainier Bancorp----------------------------------- 1
Republic Bank Corp-------------------------------- 1
Republic New York Corp---------------------- 0
Riggs National Corp------------------------------- 0
Seafirst Corp------------------------------------- 1
Security Pacific Corp----------------------- 1
Shawmut Corp (4)---------------------------- 1
Society Corp-------------------------------------- 1
Southeast Banking Corp---------------------- 1
Southwest Bancshares------------------------ 1
State Street Boston Corp-------------------- 1
Sun Banks of Florida------------------------ 1
Texas American Bancshares------------------- 0
Texas Commerce Bancshares------------------- 10
Trust Co. of Georgia------------------------ 3
Union Bank-- 0
United Banks of Colorado-------------------- 1
United Jersey Banks------------------------------- 0

```
                                            Number of
                                         Affiliated PACs
                                          June 30, 1983


U.S. Bancorp-------------------------------------- 1
United Virginia Bankshares------------------- 0
Valley National Corp------------------------- 1
Virginia National Bankshares---------------- 0
Wachovia Corp-------------------------------- 0
Wells Fargo & Co.---------------------------- 1
```

NOTES

1. Girard Bank is now owned by Mellon National Corp but is listed separately here. It will be studied, however, as part of Mellon.

2. Only one of these two PACs was listed as of June 30, 1983; therefore, the study includes only one PAC.

3. First Chicago Corp did not acquire American National Bank from Walter E. Heller International until after the 1982 election; therefore, American National Bank is not reflected here but is reflected under diversified financial services companies as part of Heller International.

4. This bank corporation established its PAC after the 1982 election and, therefore, is not included in the study.

Appendix 4

1983 *FORTUNE* 100 LARGEST DIVERSIFIED FINANCIAL SERVICES COMPANIES

Note numbers are in parentheses.

Number of
Affiliated PACs
June 30, 1983


```
Aetna Life & Casualty------------------------- 0
Ahmeanson------------------------------------- 0
Alexander & Alexander------------------------- 0
Alleghany------------------------------------- 0
American Express------------------------------ 4
American Family------------------------------- 1
American Financial --------------------------- 0
American General------------------------------ 2
American International Group------------------- 1
American Savings & Loan Assn.---------------- 0
American Savings & Loan Assn. of Florida--- 0
Baldwin-United-------------------------------- 0
Beneficial------------------------------------ 0
Beneficial Standard--------------------------- 0
Beverly Hills Savings & Loan Assn.---------- 1
Biscayne Federal Savings & Loan Assn.------- 0
Bradford National----------------------------- 0
Broadview Financial--------------------------- 0
Buckeye Financial----------------------------- 0
CIGNA----------------------------------------- 1
Capital Holding------------------------------- 0
Chubb----------------------------------------- 0
Cincinnati Financial-------------------------- 0
Citizens Savings Assn.------------------------ 1
Citizens Savings Financial-------------------- 0
City Federal Savings & Loan Assn.----------- 1
Colonial Penn Group--------------------------- 1
Combined International------------------------ 0
Continental----------------------------------- 1
Crum & Forster-------------------------------- 1
Discount Corp of New York-------------------- 0
Donaldson Lufkin & Jenrette----------------- 1
Downey Savings & Loan Assn.----------------- 0
FN Financial---------------------------------- 0
Far West Financial---------------------------- 0
Farmers Group--------------------------------- 1
Federal National Mortgage Assn.------------- 0
Fidelity Savings & Loan Assn.--------------- 0
Financial Corp of America-------------------- 0
Financial Corp of Santa Barbara------------- 0
Financial Federation------------------------- 0
First American Financial of Texas---------- 0
First Boston--------------------------------- 1
First Charter Financial---------------------- 1
First City Fed. Savings & Loan Assn.------- 0
```

Number of
Affiliated PACs
June 30, 1983

```
First Columbia Financial--------------------- 0
First Lincoln Financial---------------------- 0
First Savings Assoc. of Wisc.--------------- 0
First Western Financial---------------------- 1
Freedom Savings & Loan Assn.---------------- 0
Fremont General----------------------------- 0
GEICO--------------------------------------- 1
General Re---------------------------------- 0
Gibraltar Financial Corp of California------ 1
Gibraltar Savings Assn.--------------------- 0
Golden West Financial----------------------- 0
Great Western Financial--------------------- 1
Guarantee Financial Corp of California------ 1
Gulf United--------------------------------- 0
Hall (Frank B.) & Co.----------------------- 0
Hanover Insurance--------------------------- 0
Heller (Walter E.) International (1)-------- 2
Homestead Financial------------------------- 0
Hutton (E. F.) Group------------------------ 1
Imperial Corp of America-------------------- 1
Inter-Regional Financial Group-------------- 0
Kemper-------------------------------------- 1
Liberty------------------------------------- 1
Lincoln National---------------------------- 1
Loews--------------------------------------- 1
Lomas & Nettleton Financial----------------- 0
Marsh & McLennan Companies------------------ 0
Mercury Savings----------------------------- 1
Merrill Lynch & Co-------------------------- 1
Mission Insurance Group--------------------- 0
Monarch Capital----------------------------- 0
Naples Federal Savings & Loan Assn.--------- 0
Nevada Savings & Loan Assn.----------------- 0
Ohio Casualty------------------------------- 0
Old Republic International------------------- 0
Orbanco Financial Services------------------ 1
Orion Capital------------------------------- 0
Paine Webber-------------------------------- 1
Penn Corp Financial------------------------- 0
Prudential Fed. Savings & Loan Assn.-------- 0
Reliance Group Holdings--------------------- 1
SAFECO-------------------------------------- 1
St. Paul Companies-------------------------- 1
Sooner Fed. Savings & Loan Assn.------------ 0
Southland Financial------------------------- 1
Texas Fed. Savings & Loan Assn.------------- 1
Torchmark (2)------------------------------- 1
Transamerica (3)---------------------------- 3
Transohio Financial------------------------- 1
Travelers Corp (2)-------------------------- 1
```

```
                                       Number of
                                    Affiliated PACs
                                     June 30, 1983


United Financial Group-------------------- 0
United States Leasing International-------- 0
U.S. Fidelity & Guarantee----------------- 1
Western Casualty & Surety----------------- 0
Western Savings & Loan Assn.-------------- 1
```

NOTES

1. After 1982 Walter E. Heller International dissolved, and American National Bank became part of First Chicago Corp which is listed under bank holding companies.

2. The PAC of this corporation was established after 1982 and, therefore, is not included in this study.

3. Transamerica includes Transamerica Occidental Life which also appears on the 1983 *Fortune* 500 Largest Nonindustrials list under life insurance.

Appendix 5

1983 *FORTUNE* 100 LARGEST DIVERSIFIED SERVICE COMPANIES

Note numbers are in parentheses.

Number of
Affiliated PACs
June 30, 1983

Agri Industries-------------------------------- 0
ALCO Standard---------------------------------- 1
American Broadcasting-------------------------- 0
American Hospital Supply----------------------- 1
American Medical International----------------- 1
Amfac-- 1
Anixter Bros----------------------------------- 0
Associated Milk Producers (1)------------------ 1
Automatic Data Processing---------------------- 0
Avco--- 1
Avnet-- 0
Bally Manufacturing---------------------------- 1
Bergen Brunswig-------------------------------- 0
Beverly Enterprises---------------------------- 1
Blount--- 1
Browning-Ferris Industries--------------------- 0
CBS-- 0
CFS Continental-------------------------------- 0
Caesars World (2)------------------------------ 2
Castle & Cooke--------------------------------- 1
Centex--- 1
City Investing--------------------------------- 1
Commercial Metals------------------------------ 0
Computer Sciences------------------------------ 1
Dairymen (1)----------------------------------- 8
DeKalb Ag Research----------------------------- 0
Di Giorgio------------------------------------- 0
Dorchester Gas--------------------------------- 0
Dravo-- 1
Dun & Bradstreet------------------------------- 1
Early & Daniel Industries---------------------- 0
Eastern Gas & Fuel Associates------------------ 0
Farm House Foods------------------------------- 0
Farmland Industries---------------------------- 1
Fischbach-------------------------------------- 0
Fleming Companies------------------------------ 0
Flichinger (S. M.)----------------------------- 0
Fluor-- 2
Foremost-McKesson------------------------------ 1
Gelco-- 0
Genuine Parts---------------------------------- 0
Grain Terminal Association--------------------- 0
Grainger (W. W.)------------------------------- 0
Halliburton------------------------------------ 3
Hilton Hotels---------------------------------- 0

Number of
Affiliated PACs
June 30, 1983

```
Holiday Inns---------------------------------- 4
Hospital Corp. of America-------------------- 1
Humana--------------------------------------- 1
IU International----------------------------- 1
Interpublic Group of Companies-------------- 0
Kaneb Services------------------------------- 1
Kay------------------------------------------ 0
Landmark------------------------------------- 0
MCA------------------------------------------ 1
MGM/UA Entertainment------------------------- 0
Malone & Hyde-------------------------------- 1
Metromedia----------------------------------- 0
Morrison-Knudsen----------------------------- 1
Nash-Finch----------------------------------- 0
National Medical Enterprises---------------- 1
Nielsen (A. C.)------------------------------ 0
Nike----------------------------------------- 1
Ocean Drilling & Exploration---------------- 0
Pacific Gamble Robinson--------------------- 0
Parker Drilling------------------------------ 1
Parker Pen----------------------------------- 0
Parsons-------------------------------------- 1
Perini--------------------------------------- 0
Petrolane------------------------------------ 1
Phibro-Salomon------------------------------- 1
Pioneer Hi-Bred International--------------- 0
Pittston------------------------------------- 0
RCA------------------------------------------ 0
Ramada Inns---------------------------------- 0
Raymond International------------------------ 1
Reading & Bates------------------------------ 1
Rolins--------------------------------------- 1
Ryder System--------------------------------- 1
SEDCO---------------------------------------- 1
Servicemaster International------------------ 0
Southern States Cooperative (1)------------- 0
Subaru of America---------------------------- 0
Suburban Propane Gas------------------------- 0
Sunkist Growers (1)-------------------------- 1
Super Food Services-------------------------- 0
Super Valu Stores---------------------------- 0
Sysco---------------------------------------- 0
Tesoro Petroleum----------------------------- 1
Transway International----------------------- 0
Turner Construction-------------------------- 0
Union Equity Co-Op Exchange (1)------------- 0
U.S. Home------------------------------------ 0
Univar--------------------------------------- 0
Universal Leaf Tobacco----------------------- 0
Walt Disney Productions---------------------- 0
```

Number of
Affiliated PACs
June 30, 1983

```
Waste Management------------------------------- 1
Western Co. of North America---------------- 1
Wetterau------------------------------------- 0
Whittaker------------------------------------ 1
Zapata--------------------------------------- 1
```

NOTES

1. These companies are listed by the FEC as cooperatives, not corporations, and thus are not included in this study.

2. Only one of these PACs existed on June 30, 1983; therefore, only one is studied.

Appendix 6

1983 *FORTUNE* 50 LARGEST RETAILING COMPANIES

Number of
Affiliated PACs
June 30, 1983

ARA Services------------------------------------ 1
Albertson's------------------------------------- 0
Allied Stores----------------------------------- 0
American Stores--------------------------------- 0
Associated Dry Goods---------------------------- 0
BATUS--- 1
Best Products----------------------------------- 0
Brown Group------------------------------------- 0
Carter Hawley Hale Stores----------------------- 1
Dayton Hudson----------------------------------- 1
Dillon Companies-------------------------------- 0
Eckerd (Jack)----------------------------------- 1
Evan Products----------------------------------- 0
Federated Department Stores--------------------- 1
First National Supermarkets--------------------- 0
Giant Food-------------------------------------- 0
Grand Union------------------------------------- 0
Great Atlantic & Pacific Tea-------------------- 1
Household International-------------------------- 1
Jewel Companies--------------------------------- 1
K Mart-- 1
Kroger-- 1
Lucky Stores------------------------------------ 0
Macy (R. H.)------------------------------------ 0
Marriott-- 1
May Department Stores--------------------------- 1
McDonald's-------------------------------------- 1
Melville-- 0
Mercantile Stores------------------------------- 0
Montgomery Ward (1)----------------------------- 1
Penney (J. C.)---------------------------------- 1
Publix SuperMarkets----------------------------- 0
Rapid-American---------------------------------- 0
Revco D. S.------------------------------------- 1
Safeway Stores---------------------------------- 0
Sears Roebuck----------------------------------- 3
Service Merchandise----------------------------- 0
Sigmor-- 0
Southland--------------------------------------- 1
Stop & Shop Companies--------------------------- 0
Supermarkets General---------------------------- 0
Tandy--- 0
U.S. Shoe--------------------------------------- 0
Wal-Mart Stores--------------------------------- 1

```
                                        Number of
                                      Affiliated PACs
                                      June 30, 1983


Waldbaum----------------------------------------- 0
Walgreen----------------------------------------- 1
Wickes Companies--------------------------------- 1
Winn-Dixie Stores-------------------------------- 1
Woolworth (F. W.)-------------------------------- 0
Zayre-------------------------------------------- 0
```

NOTE

1. Montgomery Ward is affiliated with Mobil which is included on the 1983 *Fortune* 500 Largest Industrials list. It, therefore, is studied as part of Mobil.

Appendix 7

1983 *FORTUNE* 50 LARGEST LIFE INSURANCE COMPANIES

Note numbers are in parentheses.

Number of
Affiliated PACs
June 30, 1983

Aetna Life------------------------------------ 0
Aetna Life and Annuity----------------------- 0
American National---------------------------- 1
American United Life------------------------- 1
Anchor National------------------------------ 0
Bankers Life--------------------------------- 1
Charter Security Life------------------------ 0
Connecticut General Life--------------------- 0
Connecticut Mutual--------------------------- 1
Continental Assurance------------------------ 0
Equitable Life Assurance--------------------- 1
Executive Life------------------------------- 0
Franklin Life-------------------------------- 0
General American Life------------------------ 1
Guardian of America-------------------------- 0
Home Life------------------------------------ 0
IDS Life------------------------------------- 0
John Hancock Mutual-------------------------- 1
Kemper Investors Life------------------------ 0
Liberty National----------------------------- 2
Lincoln National Life------------------------ 1
Massachusetts Mutual------------------------- 1
Metropolitan--------------------------------- 1
Minnesota Mutual Life------------------------ 1
Mutual Benefit------------------------------- 1
Mutual of New York--------------------------- 1
National Investors Pension------------------- 0
National Life-------------------------------- 0
National Life and Accident------------------- 0
Nationwide Life------------------------------ 1
New England Mutual--------------------------- 1
New York Life-------------------------------- 1
Northwestern Mutual-------------------------- 1
Northwestern National------------------------ 1
Pacific Mutual------------------------------- 1
Penn Mutual---------------------------------- 1
Phoenix Mutual------------------------------- 0
Provident Life and Accident------------------ 0
Provident Mutual----------------------------- 0
Prudential----------------------------------- 2
Southwestern Life (2)------------------------ 1
State Farm Life------------------------------ 0
State Mutual of America---------------------- 0
Teachers Insurance & Annuity----------------- 0

```
Transamerica Occidental Life (1)------------ 1
Travelers----------------------------------- 1
Union Mutual-------------------------------- 1
United of Omaha Life------------------------ 0
Variable Annuity Life----------------------- 0
Western & Southern Life--------------------- 0
```

NOTES

1. Transamerica Occidental Life is affiliated with Transamerica which is included on the *Fortune* 500 Largest Nonindustrials list under diversified financial services. It is studied as part of Transamerica.

2. Southwestern Life is affiliated with Tenneco which is included on the *Fortune* 500 Largest Industrials List. It, therefore, is studied as part of Tenneco.

Appendix 8

1983 *FORTUNE* 50 LARGEST
TRANSPORTATION COMPANIES

Note numbers are in parentheses.

Number of
Affiliated PACs
June 30, 1983

```
AMR------------------------------------------------ 0
ARCO Pipeline-------------------------------------- 0
Alexander & Baldwin-------------------------------- 1
Allied Van Lines----------------------------------- 0
Arkansas Best-------------------------------------- 0
BP Pipelines--------------------------------------- 0
Bekins--------------------------------------------- 0
Braniff International------------------------------ 1
Burlington Northern-------------------------------- 1
CSX------------------------------------------------ 2
Chicago, Milwaukee, St. Paul, and---------- 1
  Pacific Railroad
Chicago & North Western Trans.-------------- 1
Consolidated Freightways--------------------- 1
Delta Air Lines------------------------------ 1
Eastern Air Lines---------------------------- 1
Emery Air Freight---------------------------- 0
Exxon Pipeline------------------------------- 0
Federal Express------------------------------ 1
Frontier Holdings---------------------------- 0
Illinois Central Gulf Railroad (1)---------- 1
Interstate Motor Freight System------------- 0
Kansas City Southern Industries------------- 1
Leaseway Transportation--------------------- 0
Mayflower----------------------------------- 0
Norfolk Southern---------------------------- 2
Northwest Airlines-------------------------- 0
Overseas Shipholding Group------------------ 0
Ozark Air Lines----------------------------- 1
PSA----------------------------------------- 1
Pan American World Airways------------------ 1
Piedmont Aviation--------------------------- 1
Purolator----------------------------------- 0
RLC----------------------------------------- 1
Republic Airlines--------------------------- 1
Rio Grande Industries----------------------- 0
Roadway Services---------------------------- 0
Santa Fe Industries------------------------- 1
Sohio Pipe Line----------------------------- 0
Southern Pacific---------------------------- 2
Southwest Airlines-------------------------- 1
Texas Air----------------------------------- 1
Tidewater----------------------------------- 0
Tiger International------------------------- 1
```

```
                              Number of
                           Affiliated PACs
                           June 30, 1983


TransWorld----------------------------------------- 2
UAL------------------------------------------------ 1
United Parcel Service----------------------- 1
US Air--------------------------------------------- 1
United Van Lines-------------------------- 1
Western Air Lines------------------------- 1
Yellow Freight System-------------------- 1
```

NOTE

1. Illinois Central Gulf is affiliated with IC Industries which is included on the *Fortune* 500 Largest Industrials list. It, therefore, is studied as part of IC Industries.

Appendix 9

1983 *FORTUNE* 50 LARGEST UTILITIES

Note numbers are in parentheses.

Number of
Affiliated PACs
June 30, 1983

Alleghany Power System---------------------- 0
American Electric Power--------------------- 2
American Natural Resources------------------ 3
American Telephone & Telegraph (1)--------- 23
Arizona Public Service---------------------- 1
Baltimore Gas & Electric-------------------- 1
Carolina Power & Light---------------------- 1
Central & South West------------------------ 4
Cleveland Electric Illuminating------------- 0
Columbia Gas System------------------------- 3
Commonwealth Edison------------------------- 1
Consolidated Edison------------------------- 1
Consolidated Natural Gas-------------------- 1
Consumers Power----------------------------- 1
Continental Telecom------------------------- 1
Detroit Edison ----------------------------- 1
Duke Power---------------------------------- 1
El Paso------------------------------------- 1
Enserch------------------------------------- 1
Florida Power & Light----------------------- 1
GTE--- 9
General Public Utilities-------------------- 1
Gulf States Utilities----------------------- 1
Houston Industries-------------------------- 1
Illinois Power------------------------------ 1
InterNorth---------------------------------- 1
Long Island Lighting------------------------ 1
Middle South Utilities---------------------- 5
Niagara Mohawk Power------------------------ 1
Northeast Utilities------------------------- 1
Northern Indiana Public Service------------- 1
Northern States Power----------------------- 1
Ohio Edison--------------------------------- 1
Pacific Gas & Electric---------------------- 1
Pacific Lighting---------------------------- 1
Pacific Power & Light----------------------- 2
Panhandle Eastern--------------------------- 1
Pennsylvania Power & Light------------------ 0
Philadelphia Electric----------------------- 1
Public Service Co. of Indiana--------------- 1
Public Service Electric & Gas--------------- 0
Sonat--------------------------------------- 1
Southern California Edison------------------ 1
Southern Co. ------------------------------- 3

```
                                       Number of
                                   Affiliated PACs
                                   June 30, 1983


Texas Eastern------------------------------------ 1
Texas Utilities---------------------------------- 4
Transco Energy----------------------------------- 1
Union Electric----------------------------------- 1
United Telecommunications------------------------ 1
Virginia Electric & Power------------------------ 1
```

NOTES

1. AT&T was about to be broken up in 1983, but this did not officially occur until after June 30. As of June 30, 1983, AT&T still had twenty-three PACs affiliated with it. Twenty of these were regional companies that were divested. For purposes of this study, only the three firms remaining with AT&T, namely, AT&T, AT&T Long Lines, and Western Electric, are included.

Appendix 10

QUESTIONNAIRE FOR CORPORATIONS WITHOUT FEDERAL PACs

<u>OPTIONAL</u>
NAME OF CORPORATION _____

NAME AND TITLE OF INDIVIDUAL COMPLETING QUESTIONNAIRE_____

If you do not wish to disclose the above information, please state the industry to which
your corporation belongs. _____

ALL INFORMATION GATHERED FROM THIS QUESTIONNAIRE WILL REMAIN STRICTLY CONFIDENTIAL.   THE
NAMES OF ALL RESPONDENTS AND THEIR CORPORATIONS WILL BE KEPT ANONYMOUS.

    I.   Does your corporation have a PAC?   (Please circle one)
        A. Yes (Please answer II only)   B.   No (Please omit II and go to III)

  II. The name of your PAC is:_____

III. What reason(s) did you have for <u>not</u> establishing a PAC?   (Please rank the reasons i
     order of importance beginning with 1.)
        _____A. Too Expensive
            _____1. To Establish
            _____2. To Administer (including reporting requirements)
        _____B. Philosophically opposed to PACs (Viewed them as corrupting)
        _____C. Fear of Alienation
            _____1. Of Employees   _____2. Of Shareholders
        _____D. Inappropriate corporate activity (Keep corporations out of politics)
        _____E. Fear of Negative Public Reaction
        _____F. Corporation Had No Need For a PAC
        _____G. Other (Please Specify)

 IV. Has your corporation previously had a PAC?   (Please circle one)
       A. Yes (Please answer V only)   B.   No (Please omit V and go to VI)

  V. What reason(s) did you have for disbanding your PAC?   (Please rank the reasons in
     order of importance beginning with 1.)
        _____A. Too Expensive
            _____1. To Establish
            _____2. To Administer (including reporting requirements)
        _____B. Philosophically opposed to PACs (Viewed them as corrupting)
        _____C. Fear of Alienation
            _____1. Of Employees   _____2. Of Shareholders
        _____D. Inappropriate corporate activity (Keep corporations out of politics)
        _____E. Fear of Negative Public Reaction
        _____F. Corporation Had No Need For a PAC
        _____G. Other (Please Specify)

 VI. Are you planning to establish a PAC?   (Please circle one)
       A. Yes   B.   No   C. Undecided

Thank you in advance for your time and consideration in completing this questionnaire.

Appendix 11

QUESTIONNAIRE FOR CORPORATIONS WITH FEDERAL PACs

NAME OF CORPORATION_____

NAME AND TITLE OF INDIVIDUAL COMPLETING QUESTIONNAIRE_____

_____

NAME OF PAC (Federal)_____ FEC# C_____

If you do not wish to disclose the above information, please state the industry to which your corporation belongs:_____

ALL INFORMATION GATHERED FROM THIS QUESTIONNAIRE WILL REMAIN STRICTLY CONFIDENTIAL.   THE NAMES OF ALL RESPONDENTS, THEIR CORPORATIONS AND THEIR PAC'S IDENTITY WILL BE KEPT ANONYMOUS.

I.   From whom does your federal PAC solicit its funds?   (Please check all appropriate categories)

_____A. Stockholders   _____C. Senior Executives

_____B. Middle Management   _____D. All Exempt Employees

        _____E. All Employees Once or Twice Per Year At Home By Mail

II. Approximately what percentage of each of the groups solicited contributes funds to your federal PAC?

A. Stockholders_____   C. Middle Management_____   E. All Employees_____

B. Senior Executives_____   D. All Exempt Employees_____

III. Which of the following solicitation methods are used by your federal PAC to obtain funds? (Please check all appropriate categories)

_____A. Letter from CEO   _____E. Postal Solicitation

_____B. Person-to-Person Appeal   _____F. Newsletters

_____C. Group Presentations   _____G. Other (Please specify)_____

_____D. Phone Solicitation   _____

IV. Which of the following persons are permitted to solicit on behalf of your federal PAC? (Please check all appropriate categories)

_____A. Supervisors   _____C. Subordinates

_____B. Peers   _____D. Other (Please specify)_____

V.   How does your federal PAC collect its funds: (Please check one, most frequently used category)

_____A. Payroll Deduction   _____C. Monthly Billing _____E. Other

_____B. Lump Sum   _____D. Pledge With Delayed Billing

VI. How is the identity of contributors to your PAC kept anonymous except for those who must be reported to the FEC? Please Explain._____

_____

VII. Are corporate guidelines provided for contributors as part of your solicitation methods?   _____1. Yes   _____2. No

VIII. Please rank the following factors related to your PAC's selection of candidates to support in federal elections. (Most important is 1)

_____A. Incumbent   _____1. Seniority   _____2. Committee Assignments

_____B. Challenger

_____C. Closeness of the Race

_____D. Likelihood of Winning

_____E. Candidates Philosophy toward Business

_____F. Candidates General Voting Record

_____G. Candidates Support by Trade Association or Pro-Business PACs that have Ranking Services (e.g. Chamber of Commerce; BIPAC)

_____H. Candidates Voting Record Only on Specific Issues of Concern to Your Industry

_____I. Other (Please specify)_____

_____

X. In what manner(s) does your federal PAC make contributions? (Please check <u>all</u> appropriate categories)

_____A. Cash to candidate or campaign committee   _____D. Loan Guarantees

_____B. Attendance at fundraisers   _____E. Other (Please specify)

_____C. In-kind contributions   _____

X. At what time(s) in an election cycle will your federal PAC make a contribution? (Please check <u>all</u> appropriate categories)

_____A. Primaries   _____C. Post-Election (e.g. Pay Off Deficit)

_____B. Pre-General Election

I. Will your federal PAC make contributions in the following situations: (Please check one <u>per</u> <u>category</u>)

A. Presidential Primaries   _____1. Yes _____2. No

B. Presidential General Election   _____1. Yes _____2. No

C. In House or Senate Contests in Districts or States Where Your Company is <u>Not</u> Physically Located   _____1. Yes _____2. No

D. To Both Sides in a Close Contest?   _____1. Yes _____2. No

E. In Response to Solicitations From Other PACs (e.g. Trade Association PACs)

                                        _____1. Yes _____2. No

F. In Races Where A Candidate is Running Unopposed   _____1. Yes _____2. No

I. Can participants in your federal PAC earmark their contributions for a particular candidate?   _____A. Yes   _____B. No

II. Which of the following group(s) participate(s) in the selection of candidates receiving support from your federal PAC? (Please check <u>all</u> appropriate categories)

_____A. Senior management   _____C. All PAC participants

_____B. Policy committee of the PAC   _____D. Other (Please specify)_____
          (Please answer XIV)

IV. Please describe the composition of your PAC's policy committee_____

_____

XV. For what period of time are the members of your federal PAC's policy committee selected?   By Whom?

      _____   _____

VI. Does your federal PAC make independent expenditures?

_____A. Yes: If so, will it make expenditures in opposition to a candidate?

         _____1. Yes   _____2. No

_____B. No (Please explain the reason(s) for this)_____

_____

VII. Approximately what cost is incurred by your corporation for administrative support of your federal PAC? _____

II. Does your corporation allow trade associations to solicit employees of your firm?

_____A. Yes   _____B. No

XIX. Does your company also have a state PAC?   _____Yes   _____No

Thank you in advance for your time and consideration in completing this questionnaire.

BIBLIOGRAPHY

BOOKS

Adamany, David W. *Campaign Finance in America.* North Scituate, Mass.: Duxbury Press, 1972.

Alexander, Herbert E. *Financing Politics: Money, Elections and Political Reform.* Washington, D.C.: Congressional Quarterly Press, 1976.

———. *Financing Politics: Money, Elections and Political Reform.* 2d ed. Politics and Public Policy Series. Washington, D.C.: Congressional Quarterly Press, 1980.

———. *Financing the 1976 Election.* Washington, D.C.: Congressional Quarterly Press, 1979.

———. *Financing the 1980 Election.* Lexington, Mass.: Lexington Books, 1983.

———, ed. *Political Finance.* Sage Electoral Studies Yearbook, Vol. 5. Beverly Hills, Calif.: Sage Publications, 1979.

———. *Political Financing.* Minneapolis: Burgess Publishing Co., 1972.

Balitzer, Alfred. *A Nation of Associations: The Origin, Development and Theory of the Political Action Committee.* Washington, D.C.: American Society of Association Executives and the American Medical Political Action Committee, 1981.

Bretton, Henry L. *The Power of Money.* Albany, N.Y.: State University of New York Press, 1980.

Cantor, Joseph E. *Political Action Committees: Their Evolution and*

Growth and Their Implications for the Political System. Washington, D.C.: Congressional Research Service, 1981.

Cigler, Allan J., and Burdette A. Loomis, eds. *Interest Group Politics.* Washington, D.C.: Congressional Quarterly Press, 1983.

*A Common Cause Guide to Money, Power, and Politics in the 97th Congress.*Washington, D.C.: Common Cause, 1981.

Corporate Political Activity. Vol. 1. Chesterland, Ohio: Business Laws, Inc., 1984.

Directory of Business-Related Political Action Committees Registered with the Federal Election Commission. Washington, D.C.: The Business-Industry Political Action Committee, 1983.

Dirty Money . . . Dirty Air?: A Common Cause Study of Political Action Committee Contributions to House and Senate Committees Review the Clean Air Act. Washington, D.C.: Common Cause, 1981.

Drew, Elizabeth. *Politics and Money.* New York: Macmillan Publishing Co., 1983.

Edsall, Thomas Byrne. *The New Politics of Inequality.* New York: W. W. Norton and Co., 1984.

Epstein, Edwin M. *The Corporation in American Politics.* Englewood Cliffs, N.J.: Prentice-Hall, Inc., 1969.

Etzioni, Amitai. *Capital Corruption.* San Diego: Harcourt Brace Jovanovich, 1984.

Fraser/Associates. *The PAC Handbook: Political Action for Business.* Cambridge, Mass.: Ballinger Publishing Co., 1982.

Greevy, David U., Chadwick R. Gore, and Marvin I. Weinberger, eds. *The PAC Directory: Book I The Federal Candidates.* Cambridge, Mass.: Ballinger Publishing Co., 1984.

———. *The PAC Directory: Book II The Federal Committees.* Cambridge, Mass.: Ballinger Publishing Co., 1984.

Handler, Edward, and John R. Mulkern. *Business in Politics: Campaign Strategies of Political Action Committees.* Lexington, Mass.: Lexington Books, 1982.

Heard, Alexander. *The Costs of Democracy.* Chapel Hill: The University of North Carolina Press, 1960.

How Money Talks in Congress: A Common Cause Study of the Impact of Money on Congressional Decision-Making. Washington, D.C.: Common Cause, 1979.

Jacobson, Gary C. *Money in Congressional Elections.* New Haven: Yale University Press, 1980.

Jacobson, Gary C., and Samuel Kernell. *Strategy and Choice in Congressional Elections.* New Haven: Yale University Press, 1981.

Johnston, Michael. *Political Corruption and Public Policy in America.* Monterey, Calif.: Brooks/Cole Publishing Co., 1982.

Kau, James B., and Paul H. Rubin. *Congressmen, Constituents, and Contributors: Determinants of Roll Call Voting in the House of Representatives.* Boston: Martinus Nijhoff Publishing, 1982.

Malbin, Michael J., ed. *Money and Politics in the United States: Financing Elections in the 1980's.* Chatham, N.J.: Chatham House Publishers, Inc., 1984.

————. *Parties, Interest Groups and Campaign Finance Laws.* Washington, D.C.: American Enterprise Institute for Public Policy Research, 1980.

Rothenberg, Stuart. *Campaign Regulation and Public Policy: PACs, Ideology, and the FEC.* Washington, D.C.: The Free Congress Research and Education Foundation, 1981.

Rothenberg, Stuart, and Richard R. Roldan. *Business PACs and Ideology: A Study of Contributions in the 1982 Elections.* Washington, D.C.: The Institute for Government and Politics of the Free Congress Research and Education Foundation, 1983.

Sabato, Larry J. *PAC Power.* New York: W. W. Norton and Co., 1984.

Schwarz, Thomas J., and Vigo G. Nielsen, Jr., Chairmen. *The Corporation in Politics 1980.* Corporate Law and Practice Course Handbook Series, No. 329. New York: Practising Law Institute, 1980.

————. *The Corporation in Politics 1981.* Corporate Law and Practice Course Handbook Series, No. 365. New York: Practising Law Institute, 1981.

————. *The Corporation in Politics 1982: PACs, Lobbying Laws, and Public Officials.* Corporate Law and Practice Course Handbook Series, No. 385. New York: Practising Law Institute, 1982.

————. *The Corporation in Politics: PACs, Lobbying Laws, and Public Officials 1983.* Corporate Law and Practice Course Handbook Series, No. 422, New York: Practising Law Institute, 1983.

Schwarz, Thomas J., and Benjamin M. Vandegrift, Chairmen. *The Corporation in Politics 1979.* Corporate Law and Practice Course Handbook Series, No. 296. New York: Practising Law Institute, 1979.

The Washington Lobby. 4th edition. Washington, D.C.: Congressional Quarterly Inc., 1982.

Weinberger, Marvin, and David U. Greevy, compilers. *The PAC Directory: A Complete Guide to Political Action Committees.* Cambridge, Mass.: Ballinger Publishing Co., 1982.

ARTICLES AND PAMPHLETS

Adamany, David. "PACs and the Democratic Financing of Politics." *Arizona Law Review*, 22, no. 2 (1980), pp. 569–602.

Alexander, Herbert E. *The Case for PACs.* Washington, D.C.: Public Affairs Council, 1983.

―――. "The Folklore of Buying Elections." *Business and Society Review,* no. 2 (Summer 1972), pp. 48–53.

―――. *PACs: What They Are; How They Are Changing Political Campaign Financing Patterns.* Booklet no. 62. Washington, Conn.: The Center for Information on America, 1979.

―――. "Political Action Committees and Their Corporate Sponsors in the 1980s." *Public Affairs Review,* 2 (1981), pp. 27–38.

"Another damper on fundraising." *Business Week,* no. 2229 (May 20, 1972), pp. 34–35.

Attitudes Toward Campaign Financing. St. Louis: Civic Service Inc., 1983.

"Bankers' Political Action Committee: One honest and effective way to participate." *ABA Banking Journal,* 72, no. 4 (April 1980), pp. 76, 79.

Baysinger, Barry D. "Domain Maintenance as an Objective of Business Political Activity: An Expanded Typology." *Academy of Management Review,* 9, no. 2 (April 1984), pp. 248–258.

Baysinger, Barry D., and Richard W. Woodman. "Dimensions of the Public Affairs/Government Relations Function in Major American Corporations." *Strategic Management Journal,* 3 (January-March 1982), pp. 27–41.

Bennett, Keith W. "PACs: Staying Afloat on the Washington Scene." *Iron Age* (July 2, 1979), pp. 36–38, 40.

Berlow, Alan, and Laura B. Weiss. "Energy PACs: Potential Power in Elections." *Congressional Quarterly Weekly Report,* 37, no. 44 (November 3, 1979), pp. 2455–2461.

BIPAC. "Business Activity in the 1980 Election: A Study of PACs Sponsored by *Fortune* 500 Companies." *Politikit* (November 1981), pp. 35–43. (Reprint)

―――. "Distribution of Contributions—The Candidate Perspective: Part Two of the *Fortune* 500 PACs and the 1980 Congressional Elections." *Politikit* (December 1981), pp. 21–30. (Reprint)

Bradford, W. Murray. "How to Get Business Heard in the Political Arena." *Price Waterhouse Review,* 23, no. 2 (1978), pp. 12–19.

Brebbia, John Henry. "First Amendment Rights and the Corporation." *Public Relations Journal,* 35 (December 1979), pp. 16–20.

Brenner, Steven, N. "Business and Politics—An update." *Harvard Business Review,* 57, no. 6 (November/December 1979), pp. 149–163.

―――. "Size Influences on Corporate Political Action Proprieties." Paper presented at the meeting of the Academy of Management, Detroit, August 1980.

"Browbeating employees into lobbyists." *Business Week*, no. 2627 (March 10, 1980), pp. 132, 136.

Buchanan, Christopher. "New Limits on PAC Contributions Advanced."*Congressional Quarterly Weekly Report*, 37, no. 42 (October 20, 1979), pp. 2337–2338.

———. "Obey—Railsback Plan Stalled in the Senate by Threat of Filibuster." *Congressional Quarterly Weekly Report*, 38, no. 1 (January 5, 1980), p. 33.

Buchsbaum, Andrew P. "Campaign Finance Re-Reform: The Regulation of Independent Political Committees." *California Law Review*, 71, no. 2 (March 1983), pp. 673–702.

Budde, Bernadette A. "The Practical Role of Corporate PACs in the Political Process." *Arizona Law Review*, 22, no. 2 (1980), pp. 555–568.

Burrell, Barbara C. "Women's and Men's Campaigns for the U.S. House of Representatives, 1972–1982: A Finance Gap?" Paper presented at the meeting of the American Political Science Association, Washington, D.C., September 1984.

"A business conduit for campaign cash." *Business Week*, no. 2419 (February 16, 1976), pp. 24–25.

"Business gains clout at the ballot box." *Industry Week*, 199, no. 1 (October 2, 1978), pp. 26, 31.

"Business money flows to Democrats." *Business Week*, no, 2454 (October 18, 1976), pp. 41–42.

"Business PACs Are Coming of Age." *Nation's Business*, 66, no. 10 (October 1978), pp. 38–41.

Calhelha, Moacyr R. "The First Amendment: Political Speech and the Democratic Process." *New York Law School Review*, 24, no. 4 (1979), pp. 921–941.

Cantor, Joseph E. "PACs: Political Financiers of the 80's." *Congressional Research Service Review* (February 1982), pp. 1–5. (Reprint)

Cathey, Paul. "Business Casts Its Vote for Political Activism."*Iron Age* (April 7, 1980), pp. 28–30.

Chappell, Henry W., Jr. "Campaign Contributions and Congressional Voting: A Simultaneous Probit-Tobit Model." *The Review of Economics and Statistics*, 64, no. 1 (February 1982), pp. 77–83.

Claude, Richard, and Judith Kirchhoff. "The 'Free Market' of Ideas, Independent Expenditures, and Influence." *North Dakota Law Review*, 57, no. 3 (1981), pp. 337–366.

Cook, Rhodes. "Fund Raising Doubles Since Four Years Ago." *Congressional Quarterly Weekly Report*, 38, no. 8 (February 23, 1980), pp. 569–571.

"Corporate Assertiveness." *Editorial Research Reports*, 1 (June 30, 1978), pp. 463–480.

"Corporate PACs: a major break with traditional policy." *Dun's Review*, 115, no. 2 (February 1980), pp. 23, 26.

"Corporate PACs Grow in Number, Influence." *Management Review*, 69 (October 1980), p. 4.

"Corporate Political Affairs Programs." *Yale Law Journal*, 70, no. 5 (April 1961), pp. 821–862.

Cox, Archibald. "Constitutional Issues in the Regulation of the Financing of Election Campaigns." *Cleveland State Law Review*, 31 (Summer 1982), pp. 395–418.

Davis, Sandra K. "The Role of PACs in the Nomination and Campaign Process." Paper presented at the annual meeting of the American Political Science Association, Washington, D.C., September 1984.

Dickson, Douglas N. "CORPACS: the business of political action committees." *Across the Board*, 18, no. 10 (November 1981), pp. 13–22.

Dooher, Patrick G., Esq. "Deductibility of Corporate Political Expenditures—Grassroots Lobbying and PACs." Reprint, pp. 3–6.

Easton, Nina. "Swimming Against the Tide." *Common Cause Magazine*, (September/October 1983), pp. 13–15.

Egan, John. "Affiliation of Political Action Committees under the Antiproliferation Amendments to the Federal Election Campaign Act of 1971." *Catholic University Law Review*, 29 (Spring 1980), pp. 713–731.

"Elections . . . Campaign Contributions." *American Bar Association Journal*, 68 (February 1982), pp. 200–201.

Elliott, Lee Ann. "Political Action Committees—Precincts of the '80's." *Arizona Law Review*, 22, no. 2 (1980), pp. 539–554.

Epstein, Edwin M. *Business and Labor in the American Electoral Process: A Policy Analysis of Federal Regulation—The Rise of Political Action Committees*. Institute of Governmental Studies, University of California, Berkeley, August 1978.

———. "The Business PAC Phenomenon: An Irony of Electoral Reform." *Regulation*, 3, no. 3 (May/June 1979), pp. 35–41.

———. "Corporations and Labor Unions in Electoral Politics." *The Annals*, 425 (May 1976), pp. 33–58.

———. "The PAC Phenomenon: An Overview." *Arizona Law Review*, 22, no. 2 (1980), pp. 355–372.

———. "PACs and the Modern Political Process." Paper presented at the Conference on the Impact of the Modern Corporation, Center for Law and Economic Studies, Columbia University School of

Law, The Henry Chauncey Conference Center, Princeton, New Jersey, November 12–13, 1982.

Etzioni, Amitai. "Is Business So Secure in a PACs Americana?"*The Wall Street Journal,* (March 20, 1984), p. 28.

Fanelli, Joseph J. "Political Action Committees." *The Corporate Director,* 1, no. 1 (January/February 1980), pp. 14–18.

Farrell, Kevin. "Do Small Business PACs Pay?" *Venture,* 5 (April 1983), pp. 98, 100.

Fletcher, Stephen H. "Corporate Political Contributions." *The Business Lawyer,* 29, no. 4 (July 1974), pp. 1071–1100.

Fox, Francis H. "Corporate Political Speech: The Effect of First National Bank of Boston v. Bellotti upon Statutory Limitations on Corporate Referendum Spending." *Kentucky Law Journal,* 67, no. 1 (1978–1979), pp. 75–101.

Freeman, Jo. "Political Party Expenditures under the Federal Election Campaign Act: Anomalies and Unfinished Business." Paper presented at the meeting of the American Political Science Association, Chicago, September 1–4, 1983.

Goldberg, Nicholas. "Shakedown in the Board Room." *The Washington Monthly,* 15, no. 19 (December 1983), pp. 14–19.

Golden, L. L. L. "A dangerous rush to political action." *Business Week,* no. 2553 (September 25, 1978), p. 14.

"The GOP's all-out campaign for Congress." *Business Week,* no. 2657 (October 6, 1980), p. 56.

Green, Mark, and Jack Newfield. "Who Owns Congress?" *Washington Post Magazine* (June 8, 1980), pp. 10–19, 21.

Grenzke, Janet. "Campaign Financing Practices and the Nature of Representation." Paper presented at the meeting of the American Political Science Association, Washington, D.C., August 30–September 2, 1984.

Holcomb, John. "Contributions Strategies of Business PACs: Industry and Regional Variations." Paper presented at the meeting of the American Political Science Association, Washington, D.C., August 30–September 2, 1984.

Holt, Michael D. "Corporate Democracy and the Corporate Political Contribution." *Iowa Law Review,* 61 (December 1975), pp. 545–579.

"How Companies Can Finance Politics." *U. S. News and World Report,* 80, no. 22 (May 31, 1976), p. 68.

Hucker, Charles W. "Corporate Political Action Committees Are Less Oriented to Republicans Than Expected." *Congressional Quarterly Weekly Report,* 36, no. 13 (April 8, 1978), pp. 849–854.

Huffman, Diana. "GM Agrees to Reveal PAC Information, Avoids Proxy Battle." *Legal Times of Washington*, 2, no. 43 (March 31, 1980), pp. 1, 6.

"Indirect Corporation Contributions Held Legal." *Congressional Quarterly Weekly Report*, 33, no. 47 (November 22, 1975), p. 2539.

Jackson, Brooks. "Business Money Flows to Rep. Gore." *The Wall Street Journal* (February 15, 1984), p. 50.

————. "Some Corporate Political Funds Consider Code of Ethics on Dealing with Legislators." *The Wall Street Journal*, (February 9, 1984), p. 27.

Jacobs, David. "Economic Concentration and Political Outcomes: Cross-Sectional and Time Series Examinations of Images of the State." Paper presented at the meeting of the Academy of Management, Dallas, August 1983.

Jacobson, Gary C. "The Effects of Campaign Spending in Congressional Elections." *The American Political Science Review*, 72, no. 2 (June 1978), pp. 469–491.

"Keep Business Cash Out of Politics?" *U.S. News and World Report*, 86, no. 17 (April 30, 1979), pp. 53–54.

Keim, Gerald D. "Foundations of a Political Strategy for Business." *California Management Review*, 23, no. 3 (Spring 1981), pp. 41–48.

Kendall, Don R. "Corporate PACs: Step-by-Step Formation and Troublefree Operation." *Campaigns and Elections*, 1 (Spring 1980), pp. 14–20.

Kensky, Henry C. "Running With and From the PAC." *Arizona Law Review*, 22, no. 2 (1980), pp. 627–652.

Kiley, Thomas R. "PACing the Burger Court: The Corporate Right to Speak and the Public Right to Hear After First National Bank v. Bellotti." *Arizona Law Review*, 22, no. 2 (1980), pp. 427–443.

Lagano, Albert S. "Elections: Corporate Free Speech—The Right to Spend and Contribute, The Right to Influence and Dominate." *Stetson Law Review*, 12 (Fall 1982), pp. 236–249.

LaMere, Joanne, and Richard Godown. "PACS: Channel for Corporate Action." *Industrial Development*, 148, no. 4 (July/August 1979), pp. 22–26.

Light, Larry, with research by Phil Duncan and Tom Watson. "Democrats May Lose Edge in Contribution from PACs." *Congressional Quarterly Weekly Report*, 38, no. 47 (November 22, 1980), pp. 3405–3409.

————. "The Game of PAC Targeting: Friends, Foes and Guesswork." *Congressional Quarterly Weekly Report*, 39, no. 47 (November 21, 1981), pp. 2267–2270.

———. "Surge in Independent Campaign Spending." *Congressional Quarterly Weekly Report*, 38, no. 24 (June 14, 1980), pp. 1635–1639.

Lydenberg, Steven D., and Susan Young. "Business Bankrolls for Local Ballots." *Business and Society Review*, no. 33 (Spring 1980), pp. 51–55.

MacWilliams, Matthew, Randall Kemp and Paul Riger. "Introducing the New Filthy Five." *Environmental Action*, 12, (May 1981), pp. 10–16.

Mager, T. Richard. "Past and Present Attempts by Congress and the Courts to Regulate Corporate and Union Campaign Contributions and Expenditures in the Election of Federal Officials." *Southern Illinois University Law Journal*, no. 2 (December 1976), pp. 338–399.

Malbin, Michael J. "The Business PAC Phenomenon: Neither a mountain nor a molehill." *Regulation*, 3, no. 3 (May/June 1979), pp. 41–43.

———. "Campaign financing and the "Special interests." *The Public Interest*, no,. 56 (Summer 1979), pp. 21–42.

Marren, Susan H. "Rediscovering the individual in federal election law." *Fordham Urban Law Journal*, 11 (Fall 1983), pp. 1057–1087.

Matasar, Ann B. "Corporate Responsibility Gone Awry? The Corporate Political Action Committee." Paper presented at the meeting of the American Political Science Association, New York, September 3, 1981.

Mayton, William T. "Politics, Money, Coercion and the Problem with Corporate PACs." *Emory Law Journal*, 29 (Spring 1980), pp. 375–394.

Mazo, Mark Elliott. "Impact on Corporations of the 1976 Amendments to the Federal Election Campaign Act." *The Business Lawyer*, 32, no 2 (January 1977), pp. 427–450.

McGrath, Phyllis S., ed. *Business Credibility: The Critical Factors.* New York: The Conference Board, Inc., 1976.

———. *Developing Employee Political Awareness.* New York: The Conference Board, Inc., 1980.

McKeown, Margaret T. Murphy. "A Discussion of Corporate Contributions to Political Campaigns." *Delaware Journal of Corporate Law*, 2, no. 1 (1977), pp. 138–145.

Middleton, Martha. "IRS Memo May Shut Some PACs." *American Bar Association Journal*, 68 (April 1982), p. 411.

Miller, William H. "Corporate PACs on Trial." *Industry Week*, 215, no. 1 (October 4, 1982), pp. 39–42.

———. "The new clout of corporate PACs." *Industry Week*, 207 (October 13, 1980), pp. 115, 118, 120.

Moore, David G. *Politics and the Corporate Chief Executive.* New York: The Conference Board, Inc., 1980.

Mulkern, John R., et al. "Corporate PACs as Fundraisers." *California Management Review*, 23, no. 3 (Spring 1981), pp. 49–55.

Nelson, Candice J. "Counting the Cash: PAC Contributions to Members of the House of Representatives." Paper presented at the annual meeting of the American Political Science Association, Denver, September 2–5, 1982.

Nicholson, Marlene Arnold. "The Constitutionality of the Federal Restrictions on Corporate and Union Campaign Contributions and Expenditures." *Cornell Law Review*, 65, no. 6 (August 1980), pp. 945–1010.

North, James. "The Effect: The Growth of Special Interests." *The Washington Monthly*, 10 (October 1978), pp. 32–36.

Perham, John C. "Big Year for Company Political Action." *Dun's Review*, 111, no. 3 (March 1978), pp. 100–102, 105.

———. "Capitalism Comes Out of the Closet." *Dun's Review*, 107, no. 2 (February 1976), pp. 47–49, 86.

———. "The New Zest of the Corporate PACs." *Dun's Review*, 115, no. 2 (February 1980), pp. 50–52.

Richards, Eric. "The Rise and Fall of the Contribution/Expenditure Distinction: Redefining the Acceptable Range of Campaign Finance Reforms." *New England Law Review*, 18, no. 2 (Spring 1983), pp. 367–394.

Rosenthal, Albert J. "The Constitution and Campaign Finance Regulation after *Buckley v. Valeo.*" *The Annals*, 425 (May 1976), pp. 124–133.

Sabato, Larry. "Parties, PACs and Independent Groups." In *The American Elections of 1982*, ed. Thomas E. Mann and Norman J. Ornstein. Washington, D.C.: American Enterprise Institute for Public Policy Research, 1983, pp. 72–110.

Saggese, A. J., Jr. "Whether Freedom of Speech Can Be Tax Deductible." *The Tax Executive*, 32, no. 2 (January 1980), pp. 152–156, 158–163.

Sendrow, Susan G. "The Federal Election Campaign Act and Presidential Election Campaign Fund Act: Problems in Defining and Regulating Independent Expenditures." *Arizona State Law Journal*, 1981, no. 4 (1981), pp. 977–1005.

Sethi, S. Prakash. "Corporate political activism." *California Management Review*, 24, no. 3 (Spring 1982), pp. 32–42.

———. "Serving the Public Interest: Corporate Political Action Strategies in the 1980's." *Management Review*, 70, no. 3 (March 1981), pp. 8–11.

Silberman, Jonathan, and Gilbert Yochum. "The market for special interest campaign funds: An exploratory approach." *Public Choice*,
35, no. 1 (1980), pp. 75–83.

"Spending smarter on political candidates." *Business Week*, no. 2661
(November 3, 1980), p. 42.

Sproul, Curtis C. "Corporations and Unions in Federal Politics: A Practical Approach to Federal Election Law Compliance." *Arizona
Law Review*, 22, no. 2 (1980), pp. 465–518.

"Survey shows respond to corporate PAC solicitation." *Political Fi-
nance/Lobby Reporter* (November 18, 1981), p. 296.

Swanson, Carl L. "Corporations and the Political Process." In *Private
Enterprise and Public Purpose*, edited by S. Prakash Sethi and Carl
L. Swanson. New York: John Wiley and Sons, 1981, pp. 355–
372.

Thoma, George A. "The Behavior of Corporate Action Committees."
Business and Society, 22, no. 1 (Spring 1983), pp. 55–58.

Vandegrift, Benjamin M. "The Corporate Political Action Committee."
New York University Law Review, 55 (June 1980), pp. 422–471.

Walker, Charles E. "Who Really Influences Congress?" *The PAC Manager* (June 29, 1984), pp. 3–4.

Walsh, Frank E. "Corporate Election Campaigns: In Conflict with the
Law or Not?" *Public Relations Review*, 9, no. 2 (Summer 1983),
pp. 7–16.

Walters, Jonathan. "PACs: Do They Buy Votes or Support a Point of
View?" *Association Management*, 35 (July 1, 1983), pp. 51–57.

"What Businesses Can Do in Politics." *Nation's Business*, 60, no. 8 (August 1972), pp. 30–32, 35.

"What You Can Do Now to Support Candidates." *Nation's Business*,
64, no. 1 (January 1976), pp. 30–31.

"Why Firms Shun Political Drumbeating." *Industry Week*, 206, no. 7
(September 29, 1980), pp. 17–19.

"Will growth in numbers dilute political action committee effectiveness?"
Cashflow Magazine, 4, no. 1 (January/February 1983), pp. 20,
22.

"Will Money Preserve GOP Gains of 1980?" *Congressional Quarterly
Weekly Report*, 40, no. 15 (April 10, 1982), pp. 814–816.

Wright, J. Skelly. "Money and the Pollution of Politics: Is the First
Amendment an Obstacle to Political Equality?" *Columbia Law
Review*, 82, no. 4 (May 1982), pp. 609–645.

PUBLIC DOCUMENTS

Code of Federal Regulations. Federal Elections. Title II. Revised as of
July 1, 1983, with amendments as of October 1, 1983.

U.S. Congress. House. Committee on House Administration. *An Analysis of the Impact of the Federal Election Campaign Act, 1972–78.* Institute of Politics, John F. Kennedy School of Government, Harvard University. 96th Cong., 1st sess. Washington, D.C.: U.S. Government Printing Office, 1979.

U.S. Federal Election Commission. *Campaign Guide for Political Committees.* January 1982.

———. "Committee Index of Disclosure Documents-(C) (1975–1976); (1977–1978); (1979–1980); and (1981–1982)." Computer printouts.

———. "Committee Index of Candidates Supported-(D) (1975–1976); (1977–1978); (1979–1980); (1981–1982). Computer printouts.

———. *The FEC and the Federal Campaign Finance Laws.*

———. *FEC Reports on Financial Activity 1977–1978; 1979–1980; 1981–1982.* Final Reports. Party and Non-Party Political Committees. Vol. III and Vol. IV. Washington, D.C.

———. *Federal Election Campaign Laws.* January 1984.

———. *Independent Expenditures.* Washington, D.C., August 1982.

———. "FEC Index of Independent Expenditures, 1977–1978, 1979–1980, 1981–1982." Washington, D.C. (1983–1984 Unofficial computer printout, March 5, 1985.)

———. "140 Index," Computer printout, June 30, 1983.

———. *Press Releases.* 1979–1984.

———. *Record,* 10, Nos. 1 and 3 (January and March, 1984).

———. *Regulations.* April, 1980.

———. "Selected List of Receipts and Expenditures-Section V-1979–1980 and 1981–1982." Computer printouts.

U.S. SUPREME COURT CASES

Buckley v. Valeo. 424 U.S. 1 (1976).
First National Bank of Boston v. Bellotti. 435 U.S. 765 (1978).

INDEX

About the Author

ANN B. MATASAR is Dean and Professor of Management at the Walter E. Heller College of Business Administration, Roosevelt University, Chicago. Previously she implemented and directed business management programs at Mundelein and Elmhurst Colleges.